SABBATH LIVING

*How Christianity Can Flourish
in the Twenty-First Century*

Phillip L. Button

PublishAmerica
Baltimore

ISBN: 1-4137-4702-7
PUBLISHED BY PUBLISHAMERICA, LLLP
www.publishamerica.com
Baltimore

Printed in the United States of America

Dedication

This book is dedicated to those persons who have experienced estrangement from religious pronouncements and actions. May whomever reads this book realize the joy of their salvation and the thrill of God's freedom in their lives.

Acknowledgments

In the five years that I have taken to write this book, my wonderful wife, Jane, has had to endure hundreds of rewrites and countless hours of listening to my "sermons." No amount of such grief should be netted out to anyone, and to you, my love, I am most grateful!

To David and Linda Snyder, who listened to each word being read and offered their valuable insights, I am deeply grateful.

Thanks to Father Robert Spriggs, PHD, who told me, "This book just has to be published. It is the foundation of religious faith."

Thanks to William Ritter, PHD, minister of the First United Methodist Church, Birmingham, Michigan, for his willingness to read several rough drafts and for his encouragement during the search for a publisher.

I thank each of my children: Pat, Jim, Mike, and Cathy; my sons-in-law, Mark and Charles; my daughter-in-law, Annie—for their willingness to participate in readings of the play. I especially thank Mark Demorest for his legal assistance and Cathy for professionally editing this book. Without their help, I could not have brought this labor of love to print.

First and foremost, I thank God for speaking to me on so many occasions in my life.

I am blessed to have Rebecca Watts as the composer of the music which is in the Jazz Musical and the final chapter of this book. Her gift of adapting my lyrics brings life and joy to the entire play and brings the focus of the book to a stunning conclusion.

CHAPTER 1

Is. 62:4

Can We Enjoy Our Lives While We Live in Beulah Land?

I had no idea what would happen to me. I confess that I was a bit unsure as to why I had gotten into this position. I was told that Jacksonville Correctional Center was a minimum security prison and, consequently, I had little to fear.

Immediately upon entering the prison, I was "shook down." This phrase, I learned, meant that I was checked for contraband. Next, I was escorted to the institution's Illinois Bureau of Identification, where my fingerprints were taken on FBI sheets and IBI sheets. This was done to see if my background included any offenses that I had not previously declared. I also was told that this would facilitate identification of my body if I were killed while in the prison. I might have bolted after that revelation, but there were five locked doors, two twelve-foot fences protected by razor wire, and many prison officials between me and the outside, or the "street," as I would soon call it. I decided to stay.

Following the fingerprinting, I posed for mug shots and sat through an extensive orientation period, which was designed to acquaint me with the many, many rules that I would be required to observe.

Finally, I was escorted to my office where, as chaplain, I would be meeting with the hundreds and hundreds of inmates who would need spiritual guidance over the years that I would serve there. If I were to tell you that as I sat in my new chair in a brand-new prison, I was full of confidence, you would know that I was lying. I was sure that every man who walked into my office would know more about the Bible than I, and I knew that helping criminals with their rehabilitation was going to be a tremendous challenge.

I quickly observed that most of the men I saw were not Caucasian nor were they the types of people who had been included in my twenty-five years of pastoral experience, my seminary education training, or my chaplaincy training. All of my experience and training had focused upon white, basically middle-class, working, mostly biblically uneducated city and farm families. Now I was meeting men who seemed more biblically educated, less formally educated, and more intense in their desire for answers than anyone I had ministered to before, men who had a common identification of convict.

What did I possess that would mean anything to them? Three of the most helpful talents I soon found that I possessed were the ability to listen, the willingness to ask questions, and the capacity to be friendly. I was told that the men I would meet would refuse to relate in a friendly manner to a nonconvict. This piece of information I quickly categorized as false. I have always found it easy to relate to children, and while these men certainly were not children, they did respond to joy, happiness, and love. I decided that these qualities would have to serve me until I could hone other skills that I would need for the long haul.

I found myself in rigorous Bible study in order to keep ahead of the hunger displayed in the questions that always seemed to come at the most unusual or inappropriate times. For instance, I would be preaching a sermon and, right at a critical point, someone would ask a question that was on his mind. I soon learned that these questions had to be answered before the truths that I had deemed important to share in the sermon would be considered.

Among the questions that I have had asked, two were asked more frequently than any others: "If Adam and Eve had only boys, where did the women come from in order for them to marry and have children?" and "Did they have intercourse with Eve?" Regardless of the sermon topic or how important the concept being shared, if I could not convincingly answer the question being asked at that moment, I probably had just dug a great hole for myself that could forever erase any credibility I desired to achieve.

The first time this happened, I swallowed and gave an answer for which I only can give God the credit. I said, "Do you believe the Bible is true?"

"Yes," the inmate answered.

I turned to Genesis 2:2 and read, "By the seventh day, God had finished the work he had been doing; so on the seventh day he rested from all work."

I then asked if anyone had had a trial. Several men raised their hands. I asked, "What does it mean when your lawyer says, 'I rest my case?'"

One of the men answered, "It means that the lawyer is done presenting his case."

I told them, "That is what God meant when He rested. All creation was done, and though all creation was not revealed at that time, it was still all done. Consequently, God did not tell us about the women who were there because it wasn't important to the story that God was telling."

I very nearly fainted at that time because I was very unsure of my competence to communicate with men whom I previously had not known. I went on with the sermon, hoping and praying that no other such questions would follow. Fortunately, I was able to finish my sermon, and I breathed a great sigh of relief.

I was told by one of the men that these questions and a few others like them are testing questions for new chaplains and volunteers who come into the prison. He said that these were ground breakers or back breakers and that I had passed the test. Somehow I knew that there would be other such tests to come.

As you begin to read this book, I want you to be aware that I am in no way asking you to compare me with a philosopher, theologian, or biblical scholar. I am not seeking to establish a new religion or to suggest that any religion or faith group is the right one or the wrong one. I am simply professing the faith that I have come to believe and, in so doing, am explaining my reasons for this belief. Hopefully you will choose to read on and possibly choose to consider adopting some of the truths that I believe are correct. If you do so, please understand that these may be dangerous to your religious comfort zone.

I confess that these beliefs have shaken my religious foundations and have inspired me to attempt to disprove them. This growth has been spiritually healthy for me; hence I have encouraged others to test some of the truths that I have discovered. Some persons have been reluctant to become engaged in conversation, while others have been extremely interested and helpful in discussing, comparing, contrasting, and even arguing their beliefs versus mine. I hope you will do me the great honor of engaging in a healthy exchange. Remember that everything I am writing may be false and misleading, or everything may be correct and true.

My involvement with men in the prison setting inspired me to investigate the central theme of belief that, if followed to its complete and total revelation, would encapsulate every truth discovery without contradiction. I did this because I observed that every religious and denominational group had its own particular set of tenets that were the truth for them. This was causing many of the inmates confusion as to what, indeed, was the real truth. As I observed the Christian faith groups and their use of the Bible, it appeared that they all were using the Bible to prove their primary creedal confessions rather than teaching biblical truths in isolation of these beliefs.

This discovery prompted me to investigate whether biblical teaching could be free of specific religious doctrine and still be relevant to the problems that these men were confronting every day in their lives. Could we who profess beliefs possibly be more interested in teaching those beliefs than in searching for the truth? Could it be possible that we were handicapping those who were seeking the truth by strapping false doctrines onto their backs? Might this confusion and compromise of the truth have a broader implication for persons throughout the world?

I began my search using various translations of the Bible and *Strong's Concordance of the Bible*. I introduced inmate participants to the method that I had chosen in order to encourage them to participate in this examination. They were warned that the study might challenge them and their beliefs. Some of the men were unwilling to participate in the program, but others took part in it.

Of course, over the last ten years many men have gone back to their communities upon release. Some of these have requested information as to how they could continue this study by engaging persons in their home churches. This is one of the reasons for this book. Other men have developed more depth in their faith to the point that they have adopted a more peaceful lifestyle. Some who have chosen not to continue have expressed the belief that the chaplain is "going to the devil."

Our goal has always been to examine every verse, every story, every myth, and, in essence, the complete Bible, primarily from a spiritual perspective. We aspired to discover any spiritual truth, whether it superseded Christian dogma or not. We attempted to read spiritually because of the direction given in John 4:24, "God is a Spirit and those that worship Him must worship in Spirit and truth." We were aware that we believed that we always had been following these instructions; however, we soon encountered the truth that we were spending too much time in physically reading and interpreting the Bible.

We concluded that any investigation either from a physical, historical, scientific, or cultural perspective, or even from the view of higher or lower criticism, can be productive only when the spiritual study is first conducted. For us this meant that the Bible is a spiritual map for an individual, a group, and for human behavioral decisions while as spiritual beings we occupy these physical bodies. For example, while historically it is interesting whether David slew Goliath, the more important study of that Scripture is for us to discover whether we are using the truth we have been given to slay the lies we are spiritually tempted to believe and, subsequently, to follow physically.

My Bible study partners and I became convinced that the Bible is an eternal repository of divine truth, reminding us of the even more spectacular truth that God has lovingly implanted in us for our walk with this perfect Creator and with each other. Without the truth of God that has been imbedded in our souls from our creation, any of the wonderful truths in the Bible would be meaningless. We are children of God by creation and by resurrection, by implantation and by petition. *cp . Jn. 1:12*

This journey has resulted in a new belief, which I have felt compelled to call Christocentric truth. Its basic components are:

> (1) God created humankind and placed humans in eternity, the boundaries of which are the Alpha and the Omega; (2) God has given humans sufficient means of knowing what is required of them; (3) When we are found not to be true to our charge by God, we are escorted through the door that has justice on one side and the blood of grace on the other, which is best explained as the Eternal Jesus Christ experience; and (4) We have been placed by God in eternity to freely live, move, and express our awareness of being God's children. *offspring* Living this truth is called Sabbath living.

In essence, Christocentric truth is God creating and saving humankind *?* prior to our actually becoming spiritual beings. God places us into the Alpha with complete freedom to use the choices provided by God for service to God and our fellow humankind. Those choices have no eternal consequences, but great temporal consequences. The components of Christocentric truth are integrally important to all who struggle with the guilt-grace problem and the greater issue of coherence of God's truth for us as related in the Bible. Consequently, in explaining this truth, I will refer to Scriptures from both the Old and New Testaments. I do not believe that there is any difference in the spiritual truths expressed in either Testament. I acknowledge that I cannot use all the Scriptures to illustrate Christocentric truth or this book would be longer than the eternity you and I have to live, however, I hope that the ones that I use will assist you in understanding this truth.

I use the Bible text because its truth is bequeathed to us as a text written in a temporal time frame with an eternal timeless setting. That means that everything in the Bible is written in the eternal present perfect tense. The eternal truth of Scripture goes beyond the Alpha and Omega. It is without beginning or ending. This truth in the Bible is God incarnate and is the experience that God desires for us to realize in our living. It is present truth in that it relates to all of God's children in the immediate as a primary guide to current daily living. And it is perfect truth as God is perfect without contradiction.

My journey in searching to find the answers to the meaning of life began many years before I became a chaplain in a prison. I guess that it began when I was about eight or nine years old. At about that time a Mr. Hal Blankenship came to my hometown, Kewanee, Illinois, and bought the local bus and taxicab business. He also joined the First Methodist Church and started a boys' choir, which I eagerly joined. I loved being in the boys' choir. Mr. Blankenship taught us to sing and enjoy the music of the church. He also would take us home in a cab or on one of his buses. We felt so very important!

While in that choir we were introduced to many hymn writers, and Mr. Blankenship would explain how these writers were sharing God's truths to us in their music. One of those writers was Charles Austin Miles, who wrote a hymn that became my favorite and has remained so to this day.

Mr. Miles wrote this hymn in about 1911, and he entitled it "Dwelling in Beulah Land." He wrote the hymn and its tune from the inspiration he received from Isaiah 62:4, "You will be called Hepzibah and your land Beulah; for the Lord will delight in you, and your land shall be married. For as a young man marries a virgin, so shall your sons marry you: and as the bridegroom rejoices over the bride, so shall your God rejoice over you."

I cannot explain to you why this particular hymn became the favorite of the boys' choir, but I do know that we begged to sing it at every practice. That choir experience is many years in the past, and I have sung thousands of songs since then, but if I were to pick one religious song to sing, I would pick that one. The wonderful eternal love expressed between God and us is, in my thinking, the cement that many of us believe is missing in our lives, and it is that cement which Miles expressed in "Dwelling in Beulah Land." In the refrain, Miles beautifully illuminated for us that eternal place in which we dwell:

> I'm living on the mountain, underneath a cloudless sky,
> I'm drinking at the fountain that never shall run dry.
> O yes, I'm feasting on the manna from a bountiful supply,
> For I AM DWELLING IN BEULAH LAND."

I get excited every time I read or sing this beautiful hymn. I am grateful that we are living eternally in Beulah Land and can never live anywhere else, because that is the only place to live. I thank God that I do not have a choice in the matter.

In Psalm 139, we are told that regardless of where we live in Beulah Land, God is with us. Unfortunately, we often believe in the illusion that we can flee from God or hide from God. The truth is that God always surrounds us. The psalmist says, "Such knowledge is too wonderful for me, too lofty for me to attain." I'm not sure that many of us would disagree with this writer.

My experience is that I want to believe the lie that sometimes I can hide under the covers and God cannot find me or see what I am doing. Miles instead says:

> Far away the noise of strife upon my ear is falling.
> Then I know the sins of earth beset on every hand.
> Doubt and fear and things of earth in vain to me are calling.
> None of these shall move me from Beulah Land.

I do not know why we ever began to imagine that we are out of Beulah Land, when there is no place else to go. We, children of God, have the ability to choose our illusions. We can pour tons of trouble into our lives and identify with it. Some of the lies that the men in prison believe are:

"I was meant to fail."

"My old man was a drunk, so I am a drunk."

"Adam and Eve put me in this stinking sewer with their illusions of grandeur, and I am stuck with the consequences. After all, didn't they get kicked out of the garden? So I guess that we are all out of luck."

"God set us up. It must have been God's will all along, or God wouldn't have put that stinking tree with its alluring fruit for Eve to eat and share with Adam."

"Didn't God give us women to get us off the track? At least God could have given us men more power to make our Eves stay at home where they wouldn't get the fruit for us to eat."

These men often separate their consciousness of the truth from their illusions and choose to believe the latter. Miles saw the problem and addressed it thus:

Far below the storm of doubt upon the world is beating.
Sons [and daughters] of men [and women] in battle long the
enemy withstand.
Safe am I within the castle of God's Word retreating.
Nothing then can reach me—'tis Beulah Land."

Miles successfully ferreted out the lie from the truth. This was the bath water that as a young child I was washed in, but I didn't realize the full extent of the blessing until I "went to prison" in 1984. What was Miles telling us in this brief sermon put in song? Let your soul listen to the beauty and truth as you read the last two verses of "Dwelling in Beulah Land."

Let the stormy breezes blow, their cry cannot alarm me;
I am sheltered here, protected by God's hand.
Here the sun is always shining, here there's naught can harm me.
I am safe forever in Beulah Land.

Viewing here the works of God, I sink in Contemplation.
Hearing now His blessed voice, I see the way he planned.
Dwelling in the Spirit here I learn of full salvation.
Gladly would I tarry in Beulah Land."

Well, I can't truthfully tell you that at nine, ten, or eleven I understood the "dwelling in the spirit" part, but around 1986 or 1987, I got a special gift from God. Soul surgery was done to my illusions. I met the truth, and the truth won!

This victory is best defined as finally understanding the entire truth of God as complete and unambiguous. Many of the explanations of God's interaction with His creation violated what I believed about God. I have always believed that God is a good God, yet many of us who are professionals in the field of religion have too often taught that God is selective in His grace.

I never have been able to reconcile how a loving God could leave out most of the world in His salvation. How could God like Europeans better than Orientals, Africans, or Native Americans? I could not handle this type of theology. I also could not understand what being baptized, taking first communion, or walking the walk of faith down the aisle had to do with making it into eternity. I was unsure how people could come to the sure belief that recruiting others would make their own entrance in the elect more assured.

So what changed? I discovered Christocentric truth. This came from several sources, as I shall explain throughout this book. A major thrust, however, came from Matthew Tindal's book *Christianity as Old as the Creation*, which was written in 1730 and reprinted only once in 1732. Reading this book, which was roundly dismissed as rubbish by the major Christian theologians, opened my eyes to God's great truth and stimulated my search into what has become unbelievably religiously exciting.

This eye-opening experience has persisted and is in high gear today—or as Jane, my wife of more than forty years, says when I shift into fourth gear in her sporty red convertible and give the turbo full reign, "You glue me back to the seat." Well, it is wonderful to be "glued to the seat" of God's eternal present perfect truth. I know that the ride is wonderful. It is "too wonderful for me."

As I am writing this, the world is trying to avoid another disaster. Thankfully this dilemma speaks to the crux of the problem we have created for ourselves in our belief that we left eternity when "Adam and Eve sinned." Look at the clock or your watch right now. What time is it? Now, mentally move to another part of the universe. What time is it where you are now? You may be answering, "It's the same time as before." Is it? The time you and I believe is correct and accurate is only an illusion for us and works only for this planet or in relation to this planet. Well, if time is an illusion, what is REAL? Everything is real as God "thinks" it or images it.

In Matthew 10:30, Jesus explains, "Even the very hairs of your head are numbered." In Genesis, we are told that we are created as God imaged us. In Revelation, we are surrounded by perfection greater than we can count if we are willing to look at the truth instead of an illusion created either by ourselves or another human (7:9).

Consider the tiny ant. If it were to attempt to ponder the ground upon which it lives and decided to measure its size and describe its characteristics, the earth likely would be measured in so many ant-lengths and be described as whatever is flat in ant language.

How many myths did we have to dismember in the twentieth century? Can you or I or anyone, for that matter, have any reality of the truth that will be old hat in the year 3000? Yet we need only to look to Deuteronomy 29:29 or 29:30 in the Jerusalem Bible, and God's truth is explained in simple yet explicit terms: "The secret things belong to the Lord our God, but the things revealed belong to us and to our children forever, that we may follow all the words of this law."

We live in a need-to-know world. God has revealed to us only the mysteries that we need to know, and those are the ones for which we are always held accountable in God's judging of our living in eternity. Think about it for a moment. If we were ever NOT in God's perfect eternity, would we be judged by God or would it be by the one whose eternity we were in? Who is the God we worship? We curse each other over whether God is a HE or a SHE, but who is God?

Much of the theology that has eschatology as one of its basic tenets stresses the theme, "You'd better watch out. You'd better not cry. Santa Claus is coming to town." And after you are judged at the "pearly gates," you will either be allowed to go in or be sent to hell for eternal punishment. There, you will have to face the devil, who will be your master.

This eschatological theology is widely believed in the Christian, Jewish, and Islamic religions. The eternal present perfect theology, which I am attempting to explain, contains no such theme. Its major statement is that God is the creator of eternity. Eternity is the truth contained between the Alpha and the Omega, the beginning and the end. *i.e. Christ alone*

As participants with God in this eternity, we are created as God has imaged us, with parameters dictated by God. There are no other realities. We are given an opportunity to express the principles God has presented to us. Among these are love, truth, peace, freedom, beauty, law, and justice. The degree to which we live these principles will determine the quality and quantity of our appreciation of and participation in God's eternity, whether we are in the soul/spiritual or in the soul/spiritual/physical states. To put this more plainly, we participate in God's eternity whether we are "in the flesh" or not. *Rom. 8:3-5*

In this book, I will refer to any lack of observance of the truth or misuse of the truth as forgetting or living the lie. Others feel more comfortable saying devil, Satan, the evil one, the beast, or Lucifer. For me, these give the lie power. God said, "There is no god but me."

Then who is God? That question is one that we all answer in some manner. Some worship God, others Allah, still others Jehovah. *Jn. 10:30*

God has so placed us in our little corner of the great Beulah Land, with our special set of toys and gadgets, in order for us to have opportunities to praise Him and our fellow occupants. As we dwell here we get evaluated, for we are accountable for all that we have been given and all the requirements that have been laid down for us. As we look around our "little corner," we find that God surely has been here. In the Old English language, there was a word that we use today in a much different manner. That word is "prevent." In Old English, prevent meant "to go before," as to go before into the room and fluff the pillows, open the windows, air out the room, and make it alive. The belief was that the air became deadly and needed to be replaced with alive air. Well, God constantly goes before us to open the door and air out our next eternal experience.

Another blessing from my youth in that Methodist Church was having Loyal Morris Thompson as minister for twelve years. He was a man who gave up professional baseball for the ministry and in the process lost his first wife, who had "married a professional baseball player, not a preacher." Dr. Thompson was an excellent pastor. He was an above average preacher who, many times, ventured into the fantastic while preaching. This was especially true on the Sunday at the beginning of baseball season when he preached his annual baseball sermon and on those frequent Sundays when he read his poetry. Since I am attempting to illustrate the Christocentric truth of the eternal present perfect, I will quote a poem of L.M. Thompson that for me illustrates this truth

> THE GARDENER GOD
> I wandered in a garden
> Among the flowers rare,
> Their garments robed in beauty,
> Their fragrance filled the air.
> Then in the peaceful stillness
> The flowers seemed to nod:
> I heard the sound of footsteps—
> It was the gardener God.
>
> I wandered in a forest
> Where trees in grandeur stood.
> There came a brooding silence
> That settled o'er the wood.
> From out of the sacred stillness
> Upon the velvet sod,
> I heard the sound of footsteps—
> It was the gardener God.
>
> I walk within a garden
> In soul transported there;

For every burden heavy
I see a flower fair.
His presence is around me
My feet bejewled shod,
Because He walks beside me—
The radiant gardener God.

How wonderful it is that God has chosen us to be aware of living in his eternity. There is nowhere else to live since we are a creation of God, yet the gift of God is our knowledge of where we are residing. The realization of this truth is in direct opposition to religious faith that partitions man's existence into a physical life, leading to heaven or hell.

God, at all times, has given humankind sufficient means of knowing what is required of us. This places upon us the responsibility of performing as per our instructions. In Genesis 1:28, humankind is told to be "fruitful and multiply."

In Genesis 2:16,[17] we are told to keep our hands off things that don't concern us, and of course in 3:16-19, God gives the consequences of inappropriate actions: judgment to these created beings. At this juncture, God declares that Adam and Eve are to leave the Garden of Eden and be transported to the east to work the ground in their physical clothing of skin (Genesis 3:21).

Whenever I ask inmates what this section means, they say that we have been kicked out of heaven. If I question them further and ask them when eternity begins for them, they will say either, "When I die" or "When judgment comes." Over the past ten years, I intentionally have asked this question of as many persons as I could, both in and out of prison, and have universally received the same answers. Somehow, we have a theology that supports the idea that God, as PERFECT, can create areas not His or Her own.

I suggest that Genesis 9:5, where we are told that God demands an accounting of our actions and activities, is more accurate. This demonstrates that instead of our being "away" from God, we are very much under the constant surveillance of God and are held accountable for all our activities. This theme is repeated in God's direction to Abraham, "by doing what is right and just, so that the Lord will bring about" what He has promised.

I will spend considerably more time with this second part of Christocentric truth in subsequent chapters. Suffice it to say at this point that the judgment of God follows our activity, and then is followed by God's forgiveness. This, for me, is analogous to the story of the lighthouse located on a rocky island. The light shines out over the waters to guide the sailors safely on their way. However, some less wise seamen dare to ignore the guidance offered them and end up crashing on the rocks. The lighthouse keepers witness the disaster and rescue the perishing seamen.

In this example, God is the light showing the way to safety, which the seamen have the freedom to follow or ignore. If they ignore the truth, they will crash. God's judgment is that the seamen have violated the truth. His justice then makes right the wrong that has been done.

This "making right" is the third part of the definition. Humankind has the freedom to follow or to ignore the truth; we do not have the power to "make right" the truth. Justice is both the doorframe and the passageway provided to the next room of God for us. Without this, we would be stuck in an impossible dilemma. However, God, being perfect in both whatever God is and in providing eternal present perfect environs, solved the obvious quandary that was presented when we were given only partial truth.

Christ is the "door" to the rest of our eternity. The idea of change is essential in God's plan of creation. It is logical to expect that God created humans who were perfect, insofar as they were given what He decided would be needed to live in eternity. God then covered this creation with His abiding presence as a kind of compass/gyroscope to reposition us effectively with the truth.

Marvin R. DeHaan, MD, in a paper that he prepared in 1988, stated:

> The blood is composed of the serum, white blood cells, and red blood cells. The serum is the substance which is composed of water, electrolytes, sugar and salt, and other elements, and also the vehicle to carry the red and white blood cells. Each white blood cell, like all other cells in the body, has a nucleus, and in it the chromosomes. The white blood cell's function is solely to ward off infection....God knew man's future need and created him with white blood cells for the time he would become vulnerable to infection. This vulnerability occurred the moment he sinned.

Thus, Christ was present at our creation and actually prior to our creation, as He is an eternal grace truth of God. At the point of our making a decision to follow the illusions or the lies we have chosen for ourselves, Christ appears as the white blood cells appear to declare our illusions false and repair the damage. Were the white blood cells not present continuously in our physical body, we would be infected beyond repair. It's like having all the doctors, nurses, hospital equipment, and medications constantly on duty.

In 1957 I worked as an inhalation therapist in Baylor University Hospital in Dallas, Texas. While there, I was privileged to view many experimental open-heart surgeries and work on helping these persons in their attempt to recover from their operations. More than 95% of these patients died following surgery because of their extreme heart problems or because corrective heart surgery was just in its infancy.

Often when one of these persons died, an autopsy was performed and I was permitted to view it. Since this was a teaching hospital, the pathologist performing the autopsy would lecture as he examined the cadaver. On one particular occasion, I remember he gave us a piece of lung to examine and said, "This man at one time had tuberculosis and didn't ever know it. This is because the body healed itself and didn't need any doctor but God."

This was a wonderful gift that pathologist and Dr. DeHaan shared from their medical experience. None of us know how many times God has stepped into our lives to give us healing, direction, comfort, and grace. Every day I give thanks to God for this gift. Jesus said, "The Lord knows your needs and meets your needs even before you ask" (Matthew 6:8). I am unaware of the number of times God has intervened in my physical life to protect me from incredible disasters, but I certainly am grateful that He has done so.

There are those of you who are asking why God didn't step in to correct or alter an event that was tragic. This apparently impossible question will be discussed and hopefully answered in the later chapters of this book.

This chapter has been designed as an introduction into Christocentric truth. I will define it in more detail in the following chapters by exploring some of the confusions that I have had in arriving at this truth and, also, by illustrating some of the confusions of our biblical ancestors.

CHAPTER 2

God, the Creator and We, the Created

My beautiful bride and I were married on a beautiful winter day. At least, that was the way it was planned to be. Yes, the weather was wonderfully warm for December 27th. The bride and groom showed up on time at the church for the ceremony, and everyone believed that this day was perfect.

Little did they know that only a few hours before, the groom-to-be had been elbow deep in grease, with tears in his eyes. He was working feverishly to remove a rusted out water plug on the side of the motor of the honeymoon car and replace it with a new one.

"Why did this have to happen to me on my wedding day," I asked myself as I tore some skin from my already bleeding fingers. "Don't I have enough to worry about with the wedding itself?" Why did I need all this confusion when I already believed that the most beautiful lady I had ever met would realize her mistake in agreeing to marry me and not appear at the wedding.

Three hours later as I stood at the front of the church and the music was playing, I looked to the closed door in the rear of the sanctuary. A cold chill was running up and down my back; I was hoping against hope that she would appear. I had dreamed a thousand dreams that she would come to the altar and agree to be my bride. I was almost afraid to breathe as I wondered, "Will that door ever swing open and, when it does, will she be there?" I wanted to run back there and call her to come to me. Finally, the doors swung open, and there she was on the arm of her father.

Again confusion enveloped my brain. "What a beautiful woman! How can I ever deserve one so wonderful? Maybe I would have been better off if she had found out what a terrible person I am, then I could slip away to some cave and disappear forever." I thought again, "I think that I am going to die right here so that she doesn't have to endure this terrible person that I am. Too late, she's at my side; her father has given his daughter to me to marry. I'd better not screw this one up. I'd better say 'Yes' and keep that promise forever."

That is the confusion that went through my mind on December 27, 1958.

Everyday, I recommit myself to honor those vows that I made that day. In spite of my many faults, my sweetheart, Janie, has loved me with a love that I can only describe as God given. She still sets my heart on fire when she walks through the door, and I still am keeping that commitment, even though I remain confused as to why I have been so blessed by God.

Marriage commitments appear to be difficult for us to fathom and to remain in for life, as we agree to do when we recite the marriage vows. If bewilderment can impact us on the level of a marriage relationship, it is even more understandable how we can be mystified when confronted with problems that require us to examine our relationship with God. In this arena, confusion can include the complete range of emotions from fear, anger, or hostility, to escape, complete resignation, and even to diminishing the size of God in our minds. This appears to be true throughout all cultures on the earth. As humans, we have a desire for a relationship with God, yet we want to understand how we can relate successfully to this Holy one whom we envision as absolute. This has led us to construct definitions of God that help to satisfy us in our quest.

In most religious cultures, God is defined in the most holy of terms. Orthodox Jews even refuse to use a name for God, instead preferring to use an attribute such as holy when referring to God. Muslims call God Allah; Brahmans call God, Parabrahm; in Egypt God has been called Thoth; early Greeks called God, Zeus. Around the world and throughout every age, we can discover humankind's reverence for their understanding of a supreme being. Christians historically have defined God in Trinitarian terms, as God, the Father; God, the Son; and God, the Holy Ghost (Spirit). This is due to the influence of long standing tradition and considerable prayer.

In Christocentric terms, I define God as the definer and the indefinable. God defines us and all creation; however, neither we nor creation are enabled to define God. In effect God is ASEITY, in that God is absolute, self-sufficient, self-organized, and self- defining. In physical terms I equate God with a sphere that is perfect in structure and form, and we receive our definition from within that sphere.

These definitions that we have given for God are the delineations that allow us, as humans, to accept our place in God's creation. Most humans believe that we have been created in some manner and by some process, and that we have been placed in this eternity by this God for some purpose.

Christocentric truth declares that God has created us and placed us within the boundaries of the Alpha and the Omega. Within these boundaries, we define ourselves as spiritual beings dedicated to serving God and each other, or committed to destroying our opportunities to do so. Yet, with these decisions uniquely confronting us, we are always within God's eternal kingdom. We are living as perfected beings by God's eternally redeeming grace, as spiritual children of God within or without the physical body. In crystal clear language, we are granted permission by God to do anything we want to do, and we remain perfect children of God.

In contrast to this, normative Christian theology confesses that we need to accept the grace of God to be saved and to gain entrance into His kingdom. Those who refuse are subjected to many opportunities to rethink their previous incorrect decisions, as long as they are alive physically. This theology is further impacted by an end times factor that serves to frighten one to repent, to confess one's sins, and to receive forgiveness. Under this theology, one's last decision is final and determines whether eternity is spent in heaven or hell.

This traditional theology is exile based and has come to us from primitive societies attempting to explain the complicated issues of life, death, suffering, pain, and our relationship to a supreme being. What is difficult for me to understand is why Judaism and Christianity chose to adopt this archaic explanation. I believe it is the basis of their misinterpretation of the prime mythological stories of Creation and the fall of Adam and Eve in Genesis.

Consider the creation myth in Genesis 1:26-27: "Then God said, 'create man in Our image, according to Our likeness'...And God created man in His own image, in the image of God He created him." Often the interpretation of this Scripture has been that we look like God except that we are not quite so big. Another explanation frequently given is that we are little pieces of God. Also, when God removed a rib from Adam to make Eve, common interpretations have Eve as inferior to Adam or at the very least a pain in the side of all mankind forevermore. Therefore, women need to subject themselves to men and speak only when given permission.

Examining the first and second chapters of Genesis Christocentrically, we need to ask for an explanation of the purpose for creation and, especially, for God's creating humans. God appears to answer that question by telling this mythical Adam and Eve to, "Be fruitful, and multiply, and replenish the earth, and subdue it: and have dominion...over every living thing." Since there is no indication that this creation had any other responsibilities, we can surmise that these commands were followed in a perfect manner. These children of God must have gone about their multiplying in an unregulated and fully compliant manner.

How long this multiplying and replenishing went on is not indicated;

however, at one point God stepped into the equation again. Here God decided to bring forth a new element. This was a special garden in the East of Eden. Here we have to explore what we are to understand as Christocentric truth by this garden's appearing at this time. When we read that God completed creation in six days, and blessed and sanctified what was created on the seventh day and then rested, we learn that all of creation was completed; however, not all of creation was revealed at that moment, but shall be revealed as God so determines.

Many have adopted the belief that the humans whom God had made began their living in this land called Eden by practicing survival skills. This demeans the character of God, for when we read the responsibilities that these people were required to fulfill, we can quickly surmise that they were very sophisticated and complicated. They had to have had language, social skills, and extensive organizational abilities. If God placed them in Eden with such extensive requirements, and there is no evidence that they were anything but successful, then are we not to assume that God also gave them the ability to intellectually grasp emerging truths and to integrate these into their existing experiences? This conclusion argues for us to have a more profound respect for God and His creation.

In the sixth chapter of Romans, Paul confessed to his difficulty in expressing the truth that he understood of God. He said, "I am speaking in human terms because of the weakness of your flesh." While writing this, I have realized the difficulty in expressing to you the glory and magnitude of God and His creation. This is due to several reasons: you and I have been taught first, that God is a personal being; second, that God exists; third, that God is three persons; fourth, that God is perfect; fifth, that God is sovereign; and sixth, that God is omnipotent.

Every one of these attributes appears on the surface to be a truth to ascribe to God because we can quote verses in the Bible to justify these statements. Remember that the Bible is for our edification. It is not for us to know more about God, but to be a guide for our decision making as we traverse the eternity God has given us. I suggest that you search yourself to discover the kind of god you want to worship and find if that god is satisfactory for your needs today. I have great difficulty in referring to God as having either human or gender characteristics; however, since I am human, I shall use anthropomorphic language, which I hope will not disturb or confuse you.

Many people struggle with present day human suffering and try to understand and believe in a God who would allow such a heinous world to exist. They can allow that there are human activities that contribute to

24

suffering and evil acts, but have problems with apparent non-god evil. Consequently, we often find apologists who are willing to "take God's side" in defense of the need for evil. They tell us such lies as: God wants to alert us to the world around us; God wants to direct us toward seeking His salvation; God wants to shape us that we may be perfect in every way; God wants to unite us by separating the sheep from the goats in preparation for His coming again; God wants to encourage us to act to help our fellow mankind who are in deeper misery than we.

If these reasons are encouragers for you to believe in and serve God, then go to it! For me and my household, we choose to affirm Christocentric truth and to reject these reasons for believing in God. We, instead, believe in a God who did create, but was never created, and who is above and beyond our most eloquent word descriptions. He gave us the ability to form these words to guide us in our expanding and ever emerging understanding of our distinct opportunities to worship this God of Gods, this King of Kings, this "I AM."

Many of us who live thousands of years later do not choose to condemn God, but hold these two mythical people, Adam and Eve, responsible for our sin problem. This affords us a greater sense of freedom in the further development of our theology. From here we are able, as "intelligent" religious theologians, to construct elaborate solutions misusing Scripture quotations to rationalize sending some persons to Hell and ourselves and others to Heaven.

As a prison chaplain, I have had men openly express their confusions about religion, the Bible, and the effect these have upon their lives. I believe that the source of their confusion comes from the training they have received from organized religion and their struggle to square this with life as they have experienced it.

Most men who are inmates have grown up in homes and church communities where biblical truths are taught as absolutes, while in life men experience inconstancies and vacillations. They have read that David was the good guy and Goliath was the bad giant, and that good always wins over bad. "How about the story of Adam and Eve? Who are the bad ones and who are the good?" they want to know. "Didn't they sin and then get kicked out of the Garden? Are we all Adams and Eves? Are we all evil and going to Hell? If that is true, who is going to Heaven?" Experience in life often does not appear as open and shut. They ask, "Does this mean that the lessons in the Bible are no longer relevant?"

For most inmates, the Bible has been the principle source of their understanding about God. They have read that God created everything from a void, including mankind. They wonder how evil can come from this god who is supposed to be only good. How can something come from nothing? Is God separate from this nothingness? Is God really a good God? They strive to dig into this unfathomable mystery by composing their own solutions, which in themselves produce additional confusion.

They question God for answers and often find only stillness. They move on to their own beginnings and struggle with the several creation stories in the Bible. They question why Adam and Eve were permitted to eat from every tree, plant, and animal on the earth except that tree which God placed in the middle of a garden. What possessed God to make this tree more pleasant to their sight than all the other trees in Eden?

Could God have provided a "set up" that made it impossible for Adam and Eve to stay in Eden? Are we also set up by God to fail? Many men observe that the total responsibility for meeting and succeeding in surmounting this challenge appears to have been placed on Adam and Eve in choosing correctly. This apparently impossible decision of Adam and Eve makes inmates wonder if they face the same result.

Let's return to that Garden and observe Eve as she walks by herself while smelling the various flowers. We can almost hear her singing the C. Austin Miles song, "In the Garden."

> I come to the garden alone,
> While the dew is still on the roses,
> And the voice I hear, falling on my ear,
> The Son of God discloses.

"Am I hearing that beautiful tree over there calling to me? It is so beautiful! I never have noticed it before. I feel that it is more lovely than any sight that I have ever seen. Shall I go over to it?" Eve asks.

> He speaks and the sound of His voice
> Is so sweet the birds hush their singing,
> And the melody that he gave to me.
> Within my heart is ringing.

Here Eve is almost in a trance because of the beauty she is experiencing. She feels dizzy, a feeling she never has had before, and one she feels difficulty in escaping. "I wish Adam were here," she hears herself whisper.

26

I'd stay in the garden with Him
Tho' the night around me is falling,
But, He bids me go; Thro' the voice of woe
His voice to me is calling.

We are told that it was Eve who was first to confront the TREE and the choice that that confrontation involved. We are shown that an outside party became involved with Eve as she was contemplating what her decision would be. This outside influence quickly entices Eve to make this most critical of choices. However, she soon learns that this outside influence will not have to bear her pain in this decision. Eve then recognizes that she needs Adam at her side. She summons Adam to the scene, and he makes the same tragic decision that his mate has made. At that point it looks as if we have a fine example of two souls sticking together through thick and thin.

They sit on the nearest rock and begin to contemplate their fate. Never before have they felt like this. These feelings cause them to feel tears running down their spiritual faces. They sense a coldness and do not have the words to describe it. These words of Tennyson appear in their minds, yet who is the one who would have determined death? What is death?

IN MEMORIAM
Strong Son of God, immortal Love,
Whom we, that have not seen thy face,
By faith, and faith alone, embrace,
Believing where we cannot prove;

Thine are these orbs of light and shade;
Thou madest Life in man and brute;
Thou madest Death; and lo, thy foot
Is on the skull which thou has made

Thou wilt not leave us in the dust:
Thou madest man, he knows not why;
He thinks he was not made to die;
And thou has made him: thou art just.

They know who made them and now the anticipation of God coming in the cool of the evening, looking for them, causes more shivering and shaking in their souls. They ask each other, "Are we now going to die? What is death? Can one live without death?"

> Thou seemest human and divine,
> The highest, holiest manhood, thou:
> Our wills are ours, we know not how;
> Our wills are ours, to make them thine.

"God always has been so kind and so loving. Is this to change? How angry will God be when He arrives to walk with us? Questions. Questions. Questions. We never have asked questions before. What does this mean? Are we going to die? What is death?"

> Our little systems have their day;
> They have their day and cease to be:
> They are but broken lights of thee,
> And thou, O Lord, art more than they.

> We have but faith: we cannot know;
> For knowledge is of things we see;
> And yet we trust it comes from thee,
> A beam in darkness: let it grow

"Here comes God now. Maybe we should hide until He sees the fruit missing from the tree. Then we can look to see if God is really angry. Oh, why did we need to eat the fruit? Why are we trying to hide? Why do we feel in need of something to cover us? What does this mean? Are we going to die? What is death? What has happened to us?" God said 'In the day you eat you shall die' They were warned.

> Let knowledge grow from more to more,
> But more of reverence in us dwell;
> That mind and soul, according well,
> May make one music as before,

> But vaster. We are fools and slight;
> We mock thee when we do not fear:

But help thy foolish ones to bear;
Help thy vain worlds to bear thy light.

"Adam and Eve, Where art thou?" called God. And he said, "I heard Thy voice in the garden, and I was afraid, because I was naked; and I hid myself ." And He said, "Who told thee that thou wast naked? Hast thou eaten of the tree, whereof I commanded thee thou shouldest not eat?" And the man said, "The woman whom thou givest to be with me, she gave me of the tree, and I did eat." And the Lord said unto the woman, "What is this that thou hast done?" And the woman said, "The serpent beguiled me, and I did eat." Genesis 3:9-13

Forgive what seem'd my sin in me;
What seem'd my worth since I began;
For merit lives from man to man,
And not from man, O Lord, to thee.

Forgive my grief for one removed,
Thy creature, whom I found so fair,
I trust he lives in thee, and there
I find him worthier to be loved.

Forgive these wild and wandering cries,
Confusions of a wasted youth;
Forgive them where they fail in truth,
And in thy wisdom make me wise.

The illusion that this couple would support each other in a distressful situation is soon dispelled when God confronts them with their failure. Adam says, in effect, "Don't blame me, blame the woman." The woman says, "Don't blame me, blame the serpent."

Here is the first example of the confusion with which we respond to God's interaction with us. The point that we have missed is not whether the fruit should have been eaten; the issue is our confusion as to who should accept responsibility for eating the fruit and for the consequences. We do not know what would have happened if each had said to God, "I made the choice to eat from the tree."

Why do we, with Adam and Eve, have such great difficulty in accepting responsibility for the choices that we make? Do we think that if we blame someone else, we will be exonerated for the crimes we commit? What tragic journeys this couple and the serpent would now experience in their expulsion from the garden. What pain and guilt we experience because of our refusal to take responsibility for our life choices.

Since Adam and Eve were so confused and unable to accept the blame for their sin, I wonder if they ever attempted to accuse God of wanting to kick them out of the garden. Maybe they should have viewed their plight as a "set up," masterminded by God. Did God feel that Adam and Eve did not meet His standards? Did He want to begin anew? Was He tired of them? Did He want to go in a different direction? Was He just trying to stir up trouble?

Possibly God had implanted an adventurous spirit within Adam and Eve to assay what their response would be to this temptation. Since God knew all the possible responses that they could make and had already compensated for every one, His tearing them away from their previous comfort zone provided them with a test to experience living and dying, good and evil, discipline and freedom.

We are Adams and Eves, created because of God's love for us, to experience his challenges. God is tempting us to choose death so that we can experience life. Unless we die to yesterday, we cannot be born to life today.

When we read the long poem of Job, we empathize with his extreme suffering. We become overwhelmed with his experiences of loss, which often causes us to question God's motives and even His righteousness. This is exactly what we should be considering when we read about this primal couple. Is God good or evil? We often are so confused by the sin of the Bible characters that we neglect to confront the primary issues.

In the final four chapters, Job encounters God and decides to absolve God of any complicity in the problems that have complicated his life. God is not so kind as to allow this chimera to continue. God confronts Job with questions relating to who is in charge of the world. God does not ask Job for forgiveness. Instead, God justifies the tests that Job has just suffered by proclaiming His omnipotence. Shouldn't Adam and Eve be ready for whatever new challenges God sends their way? Shouldn't we?

I included the poem by Alfred Lord Tennyson, IN MEMORIAM, because I find it to be especially powerful in illustrating our everlasting discomfiture with our existence. We know we are created by God; however, we are not given an eternal existence manual with which to decipher how all the pieces are going to fit together. Perhaps this is why, even today, men are unwilling to either read maps or ask for directions, or on Christmas eve read the instructions when putting together some of those impossible contraptions that Santa has left for his beloved children. It also may explain why the Eves of this world get such glee and pleasure from watching their Adams struggling to be the man in the face of their failures.

In a great and beautiful hymn, Bob Dufford, S.J., wrote:

> You shall cross the barren desert,
> but you shall not die of thirst.
> You shall wander far from safety—
> though you do not know the way.
> You shall speak your words in foreign lands
> and all will understand.
> You shall see the face of God and live.
>
> Be not afraid. I go before you always.
> Come follow me I will give you rest.

Is it possible that this may have been the message that God would have given Adam and Eve had they admitted their sin? Do you think it is possible that God may be expecting us to admit our guilt for our sins?

This terrible exchange that we read in the first part of our Bible is challenging and forms the crux of our theology. We have the "evil" problem to confront, the apparent loss of relationship with a personal, friendly god, and the impending doom of our next decisions. The confusions of our wasted youth are now the uniforms of our new stations in eternity.

As a prison chaplain, I have talked with several hundred thousand men. One of the constant themes is, "I'm not guilty because…of my mother…my father…my teacher…the neighborhood…the society…the government. After all, you want us here so you can have jobs. I am your bread and butter. Your kids wouldn't eat if I didn't come to prison."

This dilemma that men and women face in our prison system is, to my limited perspective, on a parallel with this beautiful myth in Genesis 1-3. Both Adam and Eve and the inmates are surrounded with monumental choices that affect them and their families. The complexities of these decisions often appear to be more than one can fathom at any one time. They all want to believe that, at the very least, some of the paths they walk will lead out of the maze. For the inmates, this desire is evidenced by the number of Bible studies they will attend, the number of Bibles they will accumulate, and the number of times they will submit to baptism. Yet, confession of sins and acceptance of personal responsibility is seldom considered as an option.

How nice it would be to presume that only Adam and Eve and the many sinners who end up in our jails and prison systems are the evil ones and in need of eradicating, washing, or revamping. Do we believe that these assumptions are true? Why do we resort to bizarre stereotypes when defining God's children, calling them convict, drug addict, reprobate, infidel, or pagan? How often have we looked at the outside of the pitcher and determined its worth? Do we have any idea as to what character traits will clearly identify which of us are children of God? Are we confident that God has given us perfect insight as to who will inherit God's eternity? Are we clear as to who the goats and the sheep are in Matthew 25? We read in Romans 1:18ff that God has great wrath against ungodly people. Can we egotistically believe that we can adopt this same attitude?

As a result, do we erroneously believe that we know how to separate the foolish from the wise, or those who honor God from those who espouse foolish speculations? Do we believe that we have the wisdom to separate those who exchange an incorruptible God for animals and natural creatures; those who give up their yearning for God's truth for the lusts of the body; and especially those who abandon the natural functions of sexual behavior and adopt indecent acts, such as fornication, masturbation, homosexuality, and other equally evil behavior?

The gross sin that we, as God's creation, have committed has been in adopting certain physical norms as benchmarks or shortcuts for easily distinguishing the elect from the damned. We stereotype correct religious behavior, which has led us to check the person's church attendance, her date of baptism, whether he has been circumcised, whether he follows the prescribed holy days, and which Bible she carries to church on Sunday.

As a chaplain for the past eighteen years, I have observed the feelings of condemnation that incarcerated men express as they seek to reconcile their illegal behavior. Many are uneasy even in attending church services because they do not wish to be thought of as hypocritical. They would rather be seen as "damned to Hell" than as those who get "prison religion," only to leave their Bibles at the prison gate. Others decide to attend every service that is held and get baptized at every opportunity in order not to miss out on whatever religion might be most correct. Yet, they know from previous experience that when they go back to their communities, the churches will shun them like the plague. They know that we all are caught up in Christian stereotypes of appearance and behavior.

Lew Erwin, one of my more astute Bible study colleagues, had enough of this stereotypical religious attitude and behavior as an inmate and wrote a paper illustrating the effects as he was experiencing them.

By definition, the word stereotype means to give to a person, group, or issue characteristics considered as typifying or conforming to an unvarying pattern and lacking any individuality. In reality, it is the practice of grouping entire races, classes, sexes, religions, or other bodies of people into small, narrow-minded, often unflattering descriptions.

Religious stereotyping is harmful in a number of ways. These negative depictions of a group create feelings of superiority, feelings of inadequacy, and represents the worst plague of humanity. It creates division and blindness wherever it appears, and its deadly germ infects all who come in contact with it. Religious stereotyping hurts everyone! The carrier loses the opportunity to understand the beauty of religious diversity; misses a chance to obtain knowledge of other religious cultures; and cancels any possibility of making meaningful relationships with others. The victim is demeaned, ostracized, defamed, and dehumanized. These components can sometimes lead to low self-esteem, depression, and even suicide or conversely to violence and destructive behavior. Religious stereotyping which permeates adults' thinking is usually projected onto their children. In the Bible, we are told that the sins of the fathers are heaped upon their children to the third and fourth generations.

In summary, my opinion of religious stereotyping [or as a more modern term, profiling] and the resulting disgraceful behavior is reprehensible. My regard for both lies somewhere between my regard for environmental rapists and the HIV virus. The carriers of this disease must be stopped. They should be barred from pro-creating their ideas and venomous sperm.

The chain has to be broken; religious intolerance must end if we are to survive on this planet that by the grace of God we have been placed to live.

Furthermore, the victims of these beliefs and actions must stand up and stop allowing themselves to be victims. In the Bible we read, "Have ye eyes, but see not, have ye ears, but hear not?" Let's see and hear God's truth; let's practice God's truth; let's be free!

Lew's message has a clarion ring to it, for we truly live in a sheep-goat sorting world. Using Matthew 25:31ff, we often are taught that this world is for culling the good from the bad. If you believe that is so, you are correct, but probably not in the way you have been taught. You and I were taught that we are to examine one another and to eliminate the bad, so that it does not contaminate the good.

In fact, Christians began penitentiaries to hold the goats until they were penitent and confessed that they would reform their behavior. Obviously, this form of behavior modification didn't work out as well as desired because these unrepentant sinners outlasted the money of the righteous. Finally, the government was given the task of funding these rehabilitation institutions. We still find vestiges of this philosophy in various prison systems.

In Illinois, we call them correctional centers, and we think that providing education will correct bad or illegal behavior. Long ago, wise men and women realized that there are times when education only makes smart criminals. While education is critically important, it begs the more important questions that all are related to moral issues.

Other prison experts believe that the problem of moral decay can be solved by Bible-believing pastors in our complexes. Their theme is to have visionary chaplaincy within the prison walls and fences. Expose every inmate to Jesus, and all of our problems will be solved. After all, Jesus is the answer to every problem. These do-gooders also enjoy dumping guilt on all they meet by wearing their "What Would Jesus Do" clothes and carrying their authentic King James Bibles.

Other groups of brothers wish to come into the prisons with their choirs of swaying women and "get down" with these unfortunate, innocent Afro-American men who have been sentenced by racist judges in a system that hates color. These groups believe that if they are allowed to deliver the "uncompromising Word of God" and provide ministries of counseling, then all will come to the truth. Their strategy is to present a series of lectures that their ministry members write with inspiration from the Holy Spirit. Amongst all of this do-goodism, we get additional confusion from those who profess that they are the ONLY competent, authorized persons who are able to reduce sin and evil in our prisons and in the world.

In a recently published thirty-six page declaration, Pope John Paul II reasserted the belief in the primacy of the Roman Catholic Church. He said: "[The idea that] one religion is as good as another endangers the church's mission. If it is true that the followers of other religions can receive divine grace, it is also certain that objectively speaking they are in a gravely deficient situation in comparison with those who, in the church, have the fullness of the means of salvation. We believe that this one true religion continues to exist in the Catholic and Apostolic Church" (On the Unity and Salvific Universality of Jesus Christ and the Church, 2000).

This statement brought forth those ecumenists who have optimistically believed that we possibly were in a new age of interpreting God in society in a more equanimous manner. Theologians are now reverting to square one to study if there can be compromise in order to solve the anger of the billions in this world who are disenfranchised.

As children of God, we appear to believe that we are incapable of making correct choices and, thus, must rely upon an authority figures who will make them for us. I believe that we are better off making even the wrong decisions than giving our lives over to serpentine theologies, or a church or a religion controlled by prophets, popes, ministers, pastors, or rabbis. These "experts" can suggest appropriate morals and ethics for us to follow; however, enslaving ourselves to manmade religion is fraught with too many potholes of concocted lies and assumptions.

Amazingly, even with this terrible confusion, Christians and Jews alike have demonstrated some of the most heroic and magnificent acts of kindness and mercy that can be documented throughout history. However, each also has laid the groundwork for and conducted the most heinous wars fought in the history of humankind.

When God asked the question of Adam and Eve, "What have you done?" they may have been in rebellion against God or angry toward God. Perhaps they lacked understanding, or maybe they were even complacent about God's commandments. We probably could spend a lifetime exploring which of these feelings were being expressed with their choice to violate God's command.

My excuses for my confusion could be, among others, I didn't care or I didn't understand. If I didn't care, I cannot conceive how I stood there with God and expected Him to think I was taking all of His instructions seriously.

If I didn't understand, why didn't I ask for clarification? No, I, along with all God's other children, let this moment pass without much commitment. Have I abrogated God's trust in me by casting on Adam and Eve the curse of being the progenitors of sin in the world? This not only has been my confusion, but our confusion. Haven't we had fun allowing ourselves to get off the hook by blaming them, when in effect we ought to be admitting our own guilt in this matter?

I had a clerk a few years ago who was hauling ten kilos of cocaine back to his distributors in an eastern state when he was stopped by a state trooper in Illinois for cutting in too close to a semi after passing the truck. Throughout the entire two years that I knew him, he was angry that the trooper had fabricated the reason for stopping him. He never seemed able to accept the real reason for his conviction, which was that he was indeed transporting illegal drugs. Consequently, he was angry that his wife had to sell their house because of money problems, and he couldn't look after his gravely ill mother, all because that cop decided to stop his car. Throughout the time we spent together, his confusion continued to dominate our conversations.

Of the many problems inmates in prison have recounted to me, I would definitely list confusion of the truth as being primary. Most inmates are confused as to who is guilty of the crime for which they are serving time, and they are completely mystified as to the correct pathway that will help them remain free from returning to prison.

In Galatians 4:9b-10 Paul writes, "...how is it that you are turning back to those weak and miserable principles? Do you wish to be enslaved by them all over again? You are observing special days and months and seasons and years!" We are eternal soul-spirit-mind-body children of God. We are eternal because God created us eternal; yet, everything we observe and are told is that we are finite beings who will not receive eternality until some future time. We are caught up in this confusion, which causes us to base all our judgments and decisions on this lie. Living this illusion causes us to despair and to experience disorientation.

Several years ago Sam, a man at Jacksonville Correctional Center, wrote some of his introspective thoughts for me, and I shall quote a portion of those thoughts just as he wrote them.

> Here I sit again for the twentieth time in prison. I' am caught
> in a vicious cycle of preconditioning circumstances, and weak
> will to break free. I' am deeply disturbed over my existence for

I sometime feel unhuman. I often feel fragmented, incomplete, and deeply frustrated. I have many unfullfilled voids in my soul, and they are causing me misery which often can't be seen on the out side. I feel as though I'am splitted into two persons. One side of me is very, very sensitive, emotionally, insecered, and confused. My other half is 'evil' none-caring, rebellious, and destructive. I cannot seem to really understand myself or why I do evil things, when it only hurts me emotionally and create guilty feelings. My mind is allways in a state of retrogression looking at nothing but Misery, Abuse, and Loneliness.

I listened while Sam talked of the devastating split in his understanding of truth. He was willing to work to reconcile this disfigurement of his mental and physical being, in an attempt to complement them with his spiritual truth. After about a year, he paroled from the prison and I never saw or heard from him again.

Our formal religious organizations were created to provide excellent opportunities for us to corporately live God's eternal truth; however, many of them have become tragically disastrous to our spiritual, mental, and physical health by setting their own agendas, which have been canonized as the only acceptable truth. This has happened largely because of their desire to explain evil and to delineate the solution for expunging it from the lives of sinners. However, these well-conceived efforts can cause almost schizophrenic belief systems, such as Sam's, in their followers.

Most Christian faiths have incorporated some form of a satanic belief in their theological system. Satan is considered important, not only in explaining evil, but as an instrument of God to test us. However false this may be, relative to God's eternal truth, we have adopted Satan in order not to impugn God for our sufferings in this world.

This confusion is derived from our false interpretation of the myth of Adam and Eve leaving the Garden; nevertheless, belief in the devil as God's instrument explains nothing nor does it relieve our pain of existence. For any faith to use a satanic figure in relation to God's purpose is as inexplicable as evil is in the first place. If we believe that the devil is more than God's instrument, created to explain or defuse the problem of evil from Himself, then we have a second divine power in conflict with God. If this is our faith statement, we have just changed religions and now are followers of Zoroaster.

Paul Tillich pointed out this confusion in his book *The Theology of Culture*, which cautions about our not allowing an evil ontological standing, for to do so amounts to fundamental dualism. This is the clearest antithesis to Christian faith imaginable. Yet, I can guarantee that if I lead a Bible study with inmates or in a local church and we discuss the problem of evil, the statement that the "devil has power and is active in this world" will rear its ugly head. I also can promise that no amount of argument will dispel this belief.

I believe that virtually everyone carries an element of hostility toward the confusing existence into which we have been thrown by the apparent random action of our society, parentage, and our own misdeeds. We often even believe that we have been rejected by God. We try to appease this confusing existence and, in failing, we become more and more hostile and confused. Many of us are unaware of our anger toward God. Yet, we exhibit this anger by blaming Satan or some evil force as Eve did in the Garden.

Christianity is identified as a monolithic faith, meaning that all Christians believe the same things to be truth. One of these truths, which all are supposed to collectively and universally believe, is that Jesus Christ is the Son of God. Most generally, this means that Jesus is God; however, there are those who call themselves Christian who do not believe Jesus is God. This basic division has caused schisms within the faith and even has resulted in creed declarations that have attempted to purify the faith. The leaders of the church then have been compelled by their desire to legislate this purity. This has resulted in armed troops to purge dissenters from contaminating the redeemed. This worked for many hundreds of years, however in the world of today, such actions are illegal. Excommunication is the only approved action available today.

Some might ask if I am against religion in general and Christianity in particular. The prospect of the world without religious truth is impossible, since we are inexorably attached to the umbilical cord of God; however, organized religion is both good and bad for humankind.

At its best, Christianity models the truth God has implanted in us, hence it would be grievously deficient if we were devoid of this corporate model. Many of the ravages by the things we correctly identify as evil in this world have been lessened by the peace and love that saints of Christianity have lived and shared.

Conversely, many of the horrific massacres and tortures of this world have been blessed and unleashed in the name of Christian service to God.

Where was our Christian love for the people who died in South Africa during Apartheid? To the German people after the first world war? To the Muslims during the Crusades? To diverse Christian groups in England? Scotland, and Ireland over the past one thousand years of bloody hate wars? You and I need to consider both these questions and our response in the light of our scholarship and personal experience. I have personally found distress in answering these questions when observing a new batch of inmates being processed into our prison each week. Many of us who are supposed to be professionals treat them as objects to be humiliated and debased.

Carrying this further, if an honest examination of capital punishment were pursued, could we justify the belief that relief is gained either by the condemned and his family or by the wronged and her family? Most studies have discovered that violent behavior begets more violence. How many persons do we need to kill before we have killed enough?

In our confusion, we often have falsely interpreted our purpose in this world, and our completion of that purpose, as being conditional on eventual eternal acceptance. This has necessitated our taking action in eradicating evil behavior. This process is deemed as so critical that adults believe they must implement it immediately upon our entry into the world. When these behavior modification procedures are presented to us in our early years we often comply easily.

When this method of discipline fails, punishment becomes more overt and harsh. Paddling, whipping, prison sentences, and, eventually, capital punishment are meted out as appropriate means of bringing about compliance. All of these corrective procedures are believed justified in order to prepare the sinner for God's return to earth. At that time the eternal judgment of God will condemn to hell forever all those who have refused the efforts of the "saved." Those who have received salvation will receive their reward of eternal life in heaven. While this theology builds massive churches and great cathedrals, sustains large clergy orders in pomp and regalia, and keeps massive numbers of its believers in servitude, it is a corruption of God's truth.

The coherent truth for me is Christocentric. It is eternally planted in us, His children, and contained in the Bible. We discern it coherently in the scriptures when we read spiritually, understand mentally, and live the truth physically. This is how God has directed it to be read, learned, and used: "God is Spirit, and those who worship Him must worship in spirit and trust." John 4:23-24.

As Sam has been convinced that he is a "caught" person, so we can be convinced that we are victims and find ourselves on the "devil's pitchfork," ready to accept our roasting in eternal hell. I believe that eternal hell is an oxymoron. There is only one eternity, and that is the one and only eternity created by God. cf. Ephesians. 4:1-4ff. Paul's suggestion that we should live worthy lives and cease being enticed to view ourselves as frustrated, confused, and angry might be an acceptable alternative.

Consider Psalm 23, which is usually read at the bedside of a dying person or at her funeral: "Yea, though I walk through the valley of the shadow of death, I will fear no evil: for thou art with me; Thy rod and thy staff they comfort me." While there is no reason this great truth should not be read at such occasions, we must recognize the truth of what we have just read. We are not dying. We are, in the simplest terms, leaving the soul-spiritual-physical to continue eternity without the physical. We shall only resume the physical if God decides to clothe us in it again. Does this mean reincarnation? I personally cannot conceive how God, who is perfection, needs to redo anything.

This Psalm and Galatians 4:9b-10 clearly indicate God's demand upon us to be eternally climbing mountains and walking through valleys. This, for me, precludes our having the requirement or the opportunity to redo anything. Many of us would like a second chance to hit a home run in our lives: with schooling; with spouse(s); with our children; with our parents; with our careers; etc. If I could have another chance to not eat that second, third, or fourth piece of fattening food, maybe I wouldn't be 90-100 pounds overweight. However, it's gone. It seemed to taste so good at the time. Didn't the hostess guarantee that all the fat was removed in the baking?

The writer of Ecclesiastes wrote, "I know that there is nothing better for them than to rejoice and to do good in one's lifetime; moreover, that every man who eats and drinks sees good in all his labor—it is the gift of God" (3:12-13). As I spiritually examined myself, my illusions, and my confusions, I found that I had spent a great amount of my spiritual life wishing that I were someone else or somewhere else. I discovered that I had idolized being "smart, rich, influential, handsome." All this meant that I saw myself as the opposite of each of these. In fact, even though I didn't want to admit it or prove it, I was not as I had envisioned myself. I am a child of God, a hewed-man. Hewed as God chose to fashion me. Isn't that great! God molded me, made me after His will. How tragic for me to live a life in confusion.

In Mark 6, beginning with verse 45, there is an excellent experience the disciples had that illustrates the point that we are at God's continuous beckoning. Here the disciples are ordered by Jesus to get into a boat and row across the lake to Bethsaida. While they are doing so, a storm comes up and the disciples find themselves straining against the oars to keep the boat from being swamped. This example of Jesus ordering the disciples to do an almost impossible task illustrates how God dictates the direction our lives take in the eternity God has made for us. Yet, we often live the illusion that as children of God nothing difficult is expected of us.

I suggest that our incomplete understanding of eternity has lead us to the theological quandary in which we often find ourselves. Somewhere we have gotten the idea that the time we spend on this plain of existence is a preparation for our being able to lie back in a comfortable lounge chair drinking pina coladas while enjoying a relaxing conversation with "the BIG guy."

Mark, in his gospel, has laid out a far different picture. We are created to love God and to love our neighbors as ourselves. Nothing is said about taking it easy. How much harder it is for us to love a god who expects us to perform acts of courage, one who requires us to climb mountains that never have been scaled before and to solve problems that go beyond previous understandings of truth. This can upset the apple carts of previous vendors. I think that God was not joking with the man or the woman when he commanded them to enjoy their freedom within the bounds of the sacred grove and to the limits of the perfection shared with them.

Freedom, for most of us, is a concept that means we are free from our parent God. No place is this illustrated in the Bible, nor do we experience in daily living that this freedom comes without a price. We can pretend that we can get away with living an illusion, but we always pay the price of judgment, and judgment is followed by Jesus/God's forgiving grace. We can view this eternal moment when we sin as "justice," but we can better describe it as God declaring, "Just as I see it."

God knows our transgression and moves us to another part of eternity to start over again with a new set of equations to solve in the room of our new freedom. This is what actually occurs as we move from one day to the next. However, we seldom identify it as such. Our more dramatic life-changing experiences, such as graduation from school, marriage, divorce, death of loved ones, retirement, and our own physical mortality, emphasize this change. While we can focus easily on our individual life changes, in the broader scope of community, national, and world-wide changes, we also are moved daily to make new decisions.

Sometimes we learn from our freedom, and even when we are successful in functioning within the bounds set up by God, we still are judged and are moved to a new room to begin the exploration of another area of eternity. This most definitely can be a difficult time and many of us have described this time in somewhat stumbling words as "God's Will." Eternity is best defined as a dynamic relationship between God and us. Our ride with God and each other will beat any roller coaster ride we can imagine. Thank God always that "Forever, O Lord, Thy word is settled in heaven. Thy faithfulness continues throughout all generations; Thou didst establish the earth and it stands." Psalm 119:89-90.

One of the most disturbing features of our transgressions comes about when we are convinced that we can judge for ourselves the good and the bad circumstances that we surmise to make up our eternity. Jesus cautioned us to refrain from evaluating our eternal circumstances before we have begun or completed the tour. More correctly, God directs us to serve Him and love our fellow humans and ignore judging the outcomes, as that is His responsibility and He already has judged it good. He even told us to learn from little children who, until they are corrupted by adults, accept God and expect good to come around every corner. When we become adults, we tend to view each day as a chore or as a load that we must bear.

My wife Jane has worked at a teacher at the correctional center nearly as long as I've been chaplain. One evening as we were sailing home in her convertible, she said to me, "I love expecting every day to be a great and wonderful day to serve the Lord and to love you. I also truly love going to work and teaching the men." A short time later one of her students, who has been in prison for nineteen years, came to me and spent over an hour telling me what a wonderful teacher Jane is. He described how she has, in a short time, taken him from learning basic addition and subtraction to helping him teach other men how to multiply and divide fractions. He also said that his reading has gone from a second-grade to a ninth-grade level.

We who work in prison make the choice of how we view the inmates. Many do refer to them as scum of the earth; however, we can choose to see them as God's children, creations of His perfection, fellow citizens of eternity. Unfortunately, many of these men, in their confusion, also view themselves as lost souls. One can only guess how much damage we do when we further encourage the inmates to reject themselves. How much additional hell do we want to cause them and us?

If we begin to see ourselves, our family, our friends, and, yes, even our enemies as living in the eternal present, we get to live out together the wonderful vision of God . Once convinced of this truth, our lives will seem very precious and every second will be filled with anticipation and excitement. I personally like to think of eternity as Disney World times a million. I only used a million because I can't yet imagine more joy. Please forgive me, God, for thinking so small.

As he wrote the hymn "Arise My Soul, Arise," Charles Wesley must have had just such an excitement. The knowledge that he was an eternal child of God must have kept him dancing in the streets, praising God even when the fog, rain, and filth surrounded him on every side. The words themselves are fantastic for our ears and hearts to hear even now.

ARISE MY SOUL, ARISE
Arise my soul, arise, shake off thy guilty fears;
Behold the Crucified in my behalf appears;
Before the throne my Surety stands,
My name is written in His hands;
Arise my soul, arise!

He ever lives above for me to intercede,
His all redeeming love, His precious blood to plead;
His blood atoned for the human race
And sprinkles now the throne of grace,
Arise my soul, arise!

Five bleeding wounds He bears received on Calvary,
They pour effectual prayers, they strongly plead for me;
Forgive him, oh forgive, they cry,
Nor let that ransomed sinner die.
Arise my soul, arise! Arise! Arise!

My God is reconciled, His pard'ning voice I hear,
He owns me for His child, I can no longer fear,
With confidence I now draw nigh
And Father Abba Father cry!
Arise my soul, arise! Arise! Arise!

This hymn, written in an age that was so parochial and so selective in affirming rights to all God's children, is a brilliant beacon of love and wholeness even today. In this wonderful hymn, Charles Wesley leads us as children of God to proclaim release from the sins that we have committed and that we, as guilty persons, believe are imprisoning us. He announces that we are free now to live in God's kingdom and that we are owned by God.

This is "jumping for joy" time! I can feel my soul arising, proclaiming, "Good News! Good News! Good News!" The operative word is proclaiming, since we are eternally released from our sins. Christ "has saved us and called us with a holy calling, not according to our works, but according to His purpose and grace which was given us in Christ Jesus before time began, but has now been revealed by the appearing of our Savior Jesus Christ..." 2 Timothy 1:9-10.

When I read Sam's letter, illustrating his difficulty in shaking off the despair of twenty incarcerations, I am reminded of the grievous trap that the Egyptians must have experienced as plague upon plague was visited upon them. Twenty times, Sam has come to prison; ten plagues came upon the land of Egypt. Yes, the Egyptian/Hebrew catastrophe illustrates exactly Sam's confusion. Sam wrote, "I cannot make it through a day without falling in emotions. Sometimes, I just want to hurt someone because of what I'm going through. My enthusiasm about life is very weak and often I entertain the thought of ending it. Anyone may look at me and think I'm O.K., but they cannot see the darkness that consumes me."

As I ponder Sam's and all the other inmates' problems, I am drawn inextricably to this saga of both the Egyptian's and the Hebrew's lives leading up to and through the years of these plagues. I guess it is because we have so immersed ourselves in the plague of incarceration. As citizens we continually practice the belief that the more prisons we build, the closer we get to solving our crime problems. I am continually amazed at those who believe in the "lock them up and throw away the key" philosophy.

Let's walk through this saga of the Egyptians and the Hebrews and reflect upon how, in our confusion, we are heaping live coals upon ourselves and will continue to do so until we relent from our slave-master theology. When we begin to believe Christocentrically, make decisions with timeless perspectives, and act as we have been directed in God's great commission, then we will see the end to our plagues.

Begin by picturing ourselves as Egyptians caught in a web of mistakes, and then as Hebrews with many of the same experiences, but with different reactions. Some of the sorrow and anger we, as Egyptian citizens, feel for our suffering is caused by our own stupidity and prejudice. We accept that we have treated these Hebrews worse than we would treat cows or horses. However, most of the problems have been caused by our fellow Egyptian brothers, countrymen, and leaders. We feel like victims. We cannot be held responsible for all these disasters that have been happening here in Egypt. Yet, what are we to do?

We didn't send out invitations for these nomads to stay as long as they have stayed. We know that our soldiers have killed many of those who refused to follow orders to do the work assigned; however, it is necessary to maintain peace and order. What might happen if those who have become our servants and slaves were allowed to do as they wish? How we wish they had left when the drought was over, maybe then the situation would not have deteriorated so.

Also, we have heard that these whom we now imprison have a plan that will take them home to their own land. How can we allow them to go when the economy has need of their presence to maintain itself? Won't the stock market go into the basement if we allow them to leave? We don't know what to do. Yet, look at the Nile! It's turning Red and its smell is so terrible. We can't stand it! What more can possibly happen before this whole rotten mess is finished? Why doesn't the government do something? Isn't that why we elected them in the first place?

When we, in a soul-spiritual sense, transpose ourselves into that Egyptian we need to remember the lies, the illusions, the confusion, the inept Satans we spiritually accept and worship. Do we hold such illusions? Do we feel that we are victims of the system or that the only thing we can do is to cleanse ourselves of these "bad" people? If so, do we lock them up or kill them or both? How easy it can be for us to arrive at a theology of ethnic cleansing.

Sometimes we have been successful at convincing the enemy that they are bad seed, are unsaved or lost; then we and they sink deeper and deeper into the morass of despondent, reckless, or hopeless thinking and acting. This thinking puts us on our roads to living hells; it is thinking that denies the truth given to us by God. In this confusion and illusion we believe our lies can explain all our earthly disasters, our need to hate, and our need to kill.

That is the very conclusion that caused Adam and Eve to get into so much trouble and that eventually led them to become farmers instead of gardeners. God judged them guilty and led them through the door of justice that has judgment on one side and grace on the other. They were escorted to the new opportunity made especially for them by God. Jesus said, "I am the door…" John 10:9. Jesus is the eternal door that is placed in our midst to judge our every eternal decision. We find that we are both comforted and frightened by the realization of this truth.

The predicament that we, as Egyptians, have gotten ourselves into is that we have not learned anything from any of the ten judgments sent by God. In between each door of justice, we have resented God's intrusion into the matter. This has caused us to be more and more entrenched in our false beliefs, even though each plague has been more severe than the previous one. This confrontation with God hardens our hearts. If only God had stayed out of it, we could have taken care of this problem. But, of course, God never stays out of any of our problems and decisions. Cf. Psalm 139. What does God have to do to finally get us to, "Let my people go?"

As we approach the doors we come to following our judgment/grace experiences, we obviously have learned little. Even after the tenth justice/ Jesus door is opened and shut behind us, our soldiers still are sent to pursue those Hebrews. Will we ever learn from our mistakes?

How do we relate to the catastrophe with which the Egyptians were faced? Are we willing to search within ourselves to find where we have denied our God-given truth and believed that we know better than God how eternal life should operate? As you and I spiritually open ourselves to God in our devotions, can we experience how great is our reliance upon Him and His wonderful truth?

Now, lest we be accused of being on the wrong side of the fence, let's switch to the side of the Hebrews, the Children of God fleeing those terrible soldiers. God is taking a special interest in moving the Israelites from Egypt to the land He has promised them. As we join our new friends, we share the excitement of having new blood rushing through our veins as we hear God telling Moses to "move out." Being told by God to "Get going," is both an incredible and a fearsome sensation!

As we begin crossing the Red Sea, we tremble looking from side to side and seeing that huge wall of water. Walking in that valley of the shadow of death with at least 1,300,000 persons plus all their livestock and earthly possessions, we want to ask God how He pulled this one off. This is to be a great march to the Promised Land, and we hurry to keep in step. We call to each other, "Hustle up now, so that we don't get left behind!"

God has promised that we would be provided with food, water, campsites, and everything else necessary to make the trip exciting and successful. This group has been chosen for this trip because they are the destined ones and their time has come. We have heard God say, "Rejoice, Rejoice, Rejoice!

Today is your day to experience the glory I have in store for you. Come walk with me." Upon hearing this, we walk, run, skip, jump, and float through the seabed feeling His powerful, redeeming spirit sweeping through our bodies. We are so elated that we come together and spontaneously sing what seems to be the most wonderful hymn of praise that any group could utter.

Imagine that you and I are standing with them. We sing and praise God for fulfilling His wonderful promises, for His incredible presence, and for His choosing this entire group of people to bless. Find Exodus 15 in your Bible. As you read this wonderful song, listen to the singing and the joy. Better yet, sing along with them, acknowledging the valleys that you and I have run through.

We are all so very thrilled that God has saved us from our enemies, brought us through the valley of death, and delivered us to our new safe haven. We have a God who is so unfailing in His love that He would save us in spite of our disdain for choosing to faithfully serve Him. At this brief moment of exultation, we praise God for:

> Bringing [us] in and planting [us] on the mountain of [our] inheritance - the place, O Lord, you made for your dwelling, the sanctuary, O Lord, your hands established. The Lord will reign for ever and ever (Exodus 15:17-18).

As we enjoy our arrival on the other side of the Red Sea, let us praise God, build a monument honoring Him, and celebrate, savoring this blessing of blessings. What a joy to sit for a little while and hear their stories of years of trials and unfair punishment and their progressive loss of identity. How wonderful to share the experience of their new freedom. What a joy divine to be led toward the Promised Land by so great a one as God! Happiness is everywhere!

The celebration soon must end. They and we must move on. We are in a new place with new challenges and dangers. Our children hunger and thirst. They cry for shelter from the burning sun. We cry for Moses, who is God's man, to give us water and food. The realization that we have lost our homes, our gardens, our family treasures, and our grave sites begins to overwhelm us.

With the Israelites, we begin to evaluate our present condition. Egypt really was not so awful. There were dangers, but nothing compared to what we now experience. We cry for our homes. We want to go back across the forbidden sea. We begin to curse God.

As we now fantasize about our previous life conditions, we begin to live an illusion. We even begin to envision our former enemies as our friends, and this God who we praised is now cursed.

As children of God, we have been taught that in our spiritual home abides love, truth, freedom, faith, compassion, perseverance, responsibility, courage, knowledge, and judgment. Our task is to so live in our home that God always will be honored and our fellow soul-spirits will be loved and affirmed as children of God. If we return to Egypt, will we live as God has created us? If we move on through this present difficulty, will we find a new home?

Are we so confused that we refuse to walk with God? Are we unable to lay to rest our anxiety? We need to accept the confrontation of the Master who, in His justice, declares us guilty, forgives us, and tells us to go and sin no more.

Paul, in Romans 6, warns us to refrain from sinning, for we do not need to sin to get God's grace. He tells us that God's grace abounds all around us and that we should love ourselves and each other. For many of us, accepting this truth of Christ's forgiveness appears to be too difficult. Are we afraid to realize the joy of loving and being loved?

We always are saved by the justice that is the Christ of God, because in eternity all perfection abounds. God always is removing us from our confusions, our lies, our false gods, and our deceitful activities. God eternally takes us through the Christ door that He has for us, which has judgment on one side and grace on the other. (This Grace gift will be explained more in Chapter 3.)

Many times, I watch men leaving the prison in euphoria, singing, and jumping with joy. They depart with plans for successful living. Many have written to me of those plans, saying such things as: "Chaplain, as I leave prison, I plan to get a job and to further my education. I want to become a good mechanic and to help others and tell them about Christ and His gift of his life to us." How wonderful to sing with these men as they have faced these twelve-foot fences and razor wire and now walk through it to a new start.

Too many times I have seen these same men as they have walk with stooped heads and sullen faces into a chapel service a few weeks or months later. I have heard them declare, "The devil got me within a few miles of the prison, and God saved me and brought me back to prison. If I were out there, I would be dead by now." I always have marveled at that tragically sick piece of theology. What a God to have, who would want us in prison.

Examine the exciting hymn in Exodus 15, which we sang with our brothers and sisters while we looked at the valley we had just exited. We read, "I will sing to the Lord, for he is highly exalted....The Lord is my strength and my song; He has become my salvation. He is my God, and I will praise him....our right hand was majestic in power. Your right hand, O Lord, shattered the enemy." How wonderful was the salvation revealed by God to this people, who appeared to be so desperate. These saved people, who recognized this wonderful gift of God, sing, "In your unfailing love you will lead the people you have redeemed. In your strength you guide them to your holy dwelling....You will bring them in and plant them on the mountain of your inheritance—the place, O Lord, you made for your dwelling, the sanctuary, O Lord, your hands established. The Lord will reign forever and ever."

What more affirmation of an eternal truth could there be than for this prayer to be prayed, this song to be sung? Most of us might look at this question and respond, "I only wish that in my greatest moment of deliverance, I might utter such wonderful words of gratitude to God." Yet, this hymn provides us with an excellent opportunity to compare our confusions with Christocentric theology. If the warlike statements, the insults, the murderous deprecating anger, the unabated joy at other's suffering, and the intentional celebration of being "on the right side" are spiritual uses of colorful language, then this may well be a song to be celebrated and revered.

If, however, the persons and countries appear to be references to existing persons and countries, I think that Pharaoh's army, warriors, officers, and their families would be less pleased than those who were doing the singing. In fact, were I one of the Egyptians, I would be hostile, or at the very least I would think up my own song. Maybe it is time for us to examine our spiritual singing to see if we are digging a deeper hole of confusion and lies.

Viewing this event from a distant perspective, we discover that these people called Israelites came to be in Egypt because they faced extremely hazardous conditions in their own country. Over a period of time, they migrated to Egypt to escape these problems. Whether this was the best decision for facing their impoverished conditions need not be debated. The fact is before us that resettlement was accomplished and appeared to be a fruitful decision for these tent people. They multiplied by number, by percent of the population, by possessions, and by herd and flock size.

This became a situation that was very comfortable for these nomads and very uncomfortable for the Egyptians. Consequently, the Egyptians enslaved the Israelites who had outstayed their welcome. The situation became more and more complicated. The Egyptians began to be dependent upon their unwelcome "guests," and the Israelites began to chafe under the more and more intolerable demands that were being placed upon them.

But what does one do when both sides appear locked into untenable positions? Well, God has the answer. The Egyptians, who previously wanted their guests to leave and now will not permit it, must be given strong encouragement to let go. The Israelite tribes had discovered a good thing, only to outstay their welcome. They had been placed in such bondage that they could find no way either to unite against their captors or walk away from them. Thus, they needed to get release papers.

God first appealed to both sides for some reasonable way to get this separation accomplished. However, and here we get the story that is written in the Bible chiefly from the Israelites viewpoint, neither side appeared willing to consider God's idea. The Israelite tribes were not even able to come together to march on Cairo.

Next, we have a series of disasters that we are to interpret as being principally directed at the Egyptians, but which in truth are meant to split these intertwined peoples apart. Finally, Moses convinces these tribes that they had better follow his instructions or they will suffer the plague in the same manner as the Egyptians. These unruly people listened just in time and became joined as one people. Now, we see the Hatfields on one side and the McCoys on the other. Both are convinced that the good times are definitely behind them, and it is time to do something, even if it is wrong. So, it is "get out of Dodge" time for the Israelites, and it is "round up the posse time" for the Egyptians. Moses hears God say, "Go East, young man, go East."

Now, Moses isn't all that young, but who is he to argue with God, who has been around for a lot longer than Moses? Moses gets on his camel and tells the people, "Follow me," only to find himself with the Red Sea in front of him and the armies of the Egyptians on his heels. This is one of those times when one might wish that the earth would open up and swallow one forever. Well, that's almost what happened. The sea rolled back and God kick-started Moses and the rest followed, all the time looking back in their rearview mirrors. This was one time they didn't turn to salt. They kept moving at such a pace that not only did no grass grow under their feet, they seemed to verily skim over the seabed to what appeared to be safety.

When this huddled mass of humanity, possessions, and livestock reached the East bank, they looked and wondered what would happen to them next.. They looked at each other and lamented, "Now, we will be slaughtered by the Egyptians who are coming to claim what they believe is theirs." Instead, a miracle happened, the water returned to its former position, and the "posse" was no more.

The miracle was in the minds of the Israelites only. It definitely was no miracle for God, because they were living on His eternal turf and He had control of all the conditions. Also, I sincerely believe that the Egyptian army looked on that sudden impact as a disaster. These newly freed ones worshiped God and prostrated themselves in subservience to Him. They rejoiced that they were blessed to have a God who would so pick them out of the seabed that they would be the private blessed ones in all the land.

This attitude quickly changed when they were tested by God. They didn't take kindly to Moses' telling them that they needed to heed the voice of the Lord. They grumbled against Moses and declared, "If only we had died by the Lord's hand in Egypt! There we sat around pots of meat and ate all the food we wanted, but you have brought us out into this desert to starve this entire assembly to death." This was just the beginning of what was to be a very long forty years of bickering with God and Moses by these hostile chosen people.

Let's take a few minutes to chew upon the meat that we have been fed. First, God has all the answers and will always be God, and we are God's creation. We are completely subservient to His every wish and desire. God desires and wishes, yes, even demands that we acknowledge that we are created by Him and that we can be un-created by Him at any time, in any way, and in any form. Jesus, in John 14, even declared, "I go to prepare a place for you, and if I go to prepare a place for you, I will come again and receive you unto myself."

My recognition of the truth of my complete dependence on the Lord increases my spiritual sensitivity. I have learned that, as I completely depend on the Lord, my acceptance of His guidance brings the reward of more enriched spiritual understanding. I then, in a small measure, can understand the "strong meat" of God's word, which is shared with us in Hebrews 5:14: "But strong meat belongeth to them that are of full age, even those who by reason of use have their senses exercised to discern both good and evil." Spiritual activities directed by God toward us can be very difficult for us to accept in our soul-spiritual, our soul-spiritual-mental, and our soul-spiritual-physical being.

God's truth can, in fact, be extremely tough to reconcile. When God has acted, we often have had an easier time lying to ourselves and to each other by giving the credit or blame to a devil of our own creation. However, Jesus is the one who walks us through the door, judges our lies, deceits, and transgressions on one side, and anoints us with His forgiving blood on the other. We are delivered from one room in eternity to another. At this point we can stand and curse the closed door, but this only will result in another judgment of God and another door through which we will pass.

This eternal walk with God will sometimes result in our acceptance of being chosen by God and, at other times, in our fighting against the "cross" we have been given to bear. We may live in peace in the sacred grove that God has provided, praising God for His trust in our ability to climb mountains, swim rivers, walk through valleys, or accept the millions of opportunities daily being presented by God to us. Conversely, we may curse the eternal heaven in which we abide, imagining it to be a living hell.

Often, because of our fear or cowardice, we prefer to construct devils, satans, and underworld creatures on which to vent our anger and frustrations, instead of on the only one, the Creator of all there is, the judge of all there are, and the only Savior who can restore us to singing and praising Him. In every one of these challenges, our greatest mountain to scale is praising and serving God, because in everything, whether we view it good or evil, God is providing for our GOOD!

This was exactly the problem that this now displaced group of disturbed and unhappy people exemplified following their rejoicing over their deliverance from the clutches of the Egyptians. First, they saw their problem to be the Egyptians and hated and feared them. Then, they saw their problem to be Moses and cursed him. After all, shouldn't Moses have had buses waiting there to take them directly to the Promised Land? They "murmured against Moses," causing Moses to fear for his life. Moses' distress led to a meeting between himself and God in an attempt to work out a plan to get these belligerent people through their greatest challenge. The challenge was, and still is, to accept that they were, are, and always will be in the Promised Land.

We are surrounded by many persons who would like us to experience the God whom they choose to follow and to worship. However, each of us is placed in this world to discover God in our own living and our own dying. We shall have confrontation after confrontation that will stir us to the very core of our existence. We may ask, "Why?" Yet, that is almost always answered with, "Why not?" God wants us to face life on the terms that He lays out for us, and these terms are different for each of us.

Many times in our short physical lives we will need to decide what being a child of God means and what is required of us. We can attempt to deny that we are even interested in the exercise, yet God always explodes into our spiritual psyche and confronts us with impossible dilemmas, which we cannot ignore or dismiss. God takes us to the timber lines of our lives and exposes us to scars and twisted limbs.

My friend and mentor, Dr. Loyal Thompson, wrote of this experience in the following poem:

DOGGED SERENITY
O lone, scarred monarch
By the great river's side
Thou hast battled thy foes,
The winds and the tide,
In the clash of the years
How great is thy loss!
They have broken thy form
To an old, rough hewn cross;

The fierce, lurid fires
Have seared thy heart
While the swift jagged lightening
Would rend thee apart:
Though broken in form
Thou dost stand grandly true,
With dogged serenity
Growing anew.

When the fate of the years
Shall at last come to thee,
I pray that thy mantle
May fall upon me.

Yes, we may become gnarled, storm tested, and broken. The years may indeed play havoc with our physical and mental lives. God is the one who does the testing, and the real question for us to answer is will we still be praying, "Thy will be done?" Can we witness our faith as did that great Christian of the seventeenth century, Blaise Pascal? Suffering with cancer, he prayed:

> I ask you neither for health nor sickness, for life nor for death; but that you manage my health and sickness, my life and death, for your glory. You alone know what is necessary for me; you are the sovereign master; do with me according to your will. Give to me, or take away from me, only conform my will to yours. I know but one thing, Lord, that it is good to follow you and bad to offend you. Apart from that, I don't know what is good or bad in anything. I don't know which is most profitable to me, health or sickness, wealth or poverty, nor anything else in the world. This discernment is beyond the power of men and is hidden among the secrets of your Providence, which I adore, but do not seek to measure.

CHAPTER 3
Christ-God: Eternal Life-Knowledge-Faith

"Who do people say that the Son of Man is?" was the question that Jesus asked His disciples when they were in Caesarea Philippi. We, who call ourselves Christians, must also answer this question at some period in our lives because it is central to the faith. Some are able only to refer to Jesus as the Son of God, while most Christians believe that He is God Incarnate.

The answer to this question became the definitive reason for the Council of Nicea, which adopted a creed intended to separate orthodox Christians from heretical groups. Today, we have a more difficult time with answers to such questions, and we often find our eyes glazing over when someone even tries to explain the importance of councils such as these in the early days of Christendom.

If we had been alive and believers in the early centuries of the Christian religion, we would have been more than interested in our faith, we would have been fanatical. We would have joined other like believers and fought to test persons to determine if they were "Of the Faith." Most of us would have known persons who had died for the religion we cherished, and we might have been asked also to offer ourselves to take up our cross and die.

Among the stories demonstrating this fanaticism is the story of the baptism of King Aengus by Saint Patrick in the fifth century. During the baptism, St. Patrick leaned on his sharp-pointed staff and inadvertently stabbed the king's foot. After the baptism was over Patrick looked down and saw the blood. Realizing what he had done, he begged the king's forgiveness. "Why did you suffer in silence?" Patrick asked his king. The king replied, "I thought it was part of the ritual."

We may have made such statements about suffering or dying for God as part of our confirmation service. However, do we expect to have this commitment take on a serious meaning? Many times in the hundreds of years since Christ was resurrected, that very demand has been made of dedicated men and women.

In the very century that Christ ascended from earth, hundreds of men and women chose to suffer painful executions for the faith they realized was critical to life. The Apostle Paul was willing to tell us of his suffering and imprisonments in order that we would be aware of the life that might be in store for us as we took up our crosses. The pain of professing our faith continued far beyond the time of Paul.

Any student of the Christian faith can easily find martyrs who preferred to die rather than to renounce their allegiance to Christ. This especially was true of the period called the Crusades, which lasted from about 1100 A.D. to about 1300 A.D. This period of taking up the cross of Christ was directed against persons of the Islamic faith.

The Muslim belief system was decried as being so heathen that Christians must choose to fight and even die to demonstrate their faithfulness to God. The Christian people were led to believe that God was demanding His followers to clear the world of infidels so that He could return to Earth. In retrospect, we now are able to identify that there also were other reasons for that bloody period.

Have we, as Christians, learned anything from our fighting and dying? I believe that we learned that if we are going to die, we need to identify our suffering with our faith. Consequently, we have continued dying even throughout the twentieth century and are having only minor difficulty in not identifying our current worldwide conflict with the terrorists as a religious war.

Christian men in prison often confess that their lives have been filled with suffering and imprisonment because of the call of Jesus. They evaluate the harassment they receive while in prison, the terrible crime-infested neighborhoods in which they must live, and the evil they experience upon their release as the devils they must overcome in order to prove their love for Christ.

We, who have not shared their experiences, believe that we have matured and are free from these fanatical activities and beliefs. When questioned, we confess that adornment such as crosses, badges, and head coverings are worn only to balance out an outfit or to make a simple statement of our faith. Our flags, pledges, and confessions identify us with like-minded believers and remind us that we shall survive life's obstacles. We normally are not stating that we are obliged to defend the faith with our lives.

Western religions appear to have developed their faith around threatening and being threatened. In fact, those groups that have the greatest growth vitality are those that are dealing with external threat. Many in the Catholic church believe it was strongest when at war with Muslims or Protestants. Muslims and Jews have often identified their greatest eras as including the expelling of their enemies from sacred territories.

Today, we observe Pentecostalists, fundamentalists, and extremely conservative Catholics enjoying vitality and growth in numbers of converts as they adopt the mantra of declaring war on the enemies of God. While they no longer are advocating murder or religious cleansing, the rhetoric they adopt certainly energizes the faithful to exterminate unbelievers with spiritual exhortations and to repair new converts with the oil of contrition and the blessing of holiness.

Such groups often appear energized when they discover enclaves of disparate believers. Why are believers strengthened by an external threat? Most believe that the threat reminds one of life and death expectations. Consequently, leaders are expected to identify impending doom and to lead the faithful in defeating the enemy, Satan.

Can religion ever be lived free from this external threat as its raison d'etre? Probably we will be experiencing this confusion during our entire journey through our Alpha-Omega eternity. There have been three recent examples of this good-against-evil conflict. The first is the Palestinian Muslim view versus the Jewish religious view concerning who should occupy the Holy Land. Next is the conflict between Western civilizations and the Japanese, which resulted in our adopting World War II as a religious cause. Last is the abortive conflicts in Korea and Indochina in which our national leadership failed to properly convince the religious community of their theological importance.

Three recently discovered communities appear to have realized a religion free from this conflict. They are the Hawaiians prior to the invasion by the Europeans, the Australian Aborigines before the European prisoners were dumped there, and the Eskimos in Alaska. These communities have had religious societies that are almost entirely free from warlike theologies.

Are Christianity and its mother religion, Judaism, authentic only when at war against all other faiths? Could those who interpreted the foundations of the "chosen" faith have heaped burning coals upon our heads and caused us to be immersed in confusion? Could we be living in anger against others because of "the sins of our fathers" by falsely interpreting God's truth? Does God need us to defend Him?

In Deuteronomy 32:4 we have this message stated explicitly: "He [God] is the Rock, his work is perfect: for all his ways are judgment: a God of truth and without iniquity, just and right is he." I believe that this verse is the cornerstone of our existence and our salvation. Without a coherent creation, we would have no truth upon which to base further revelations. Living within this perfect creation, we are given life. Life is freedom to love or to despise God without the need to fear annihilation. Life is freedom with judgment and salvation from the Christ/God. Without life, we have no need for perfection, judgment, or salvation.

We have this truth illustrated in the book of Job. For most of the book Job has suffered countless devastating problems. Finally, God appears before Job and questions him about those problems. Job tells of his faithfulness. In his forthrightness, he pushes the envelope as he responds to God. And God says: "Brace yourself like a man; I will question you, and you shall answer me. Where were you when I laid the earth's foundation? Tell me, if you understand. Who marked off its dimensions? Surely you know! Who stretched a measuring line across it? On what were its footings set, or who laid its cornerstone—while the morning stars sang together and all the angels shouted for joy?" (Job 38:3ff.)

Here Job receives God's judgment. If Job were not free to dishonor God, he would not have had the gift of life and this interchange would be irrelevant for us.

When Jesus came along hundreds of years later, He understandably wanted His followers to make decisions that would express their allegiance either to Him or His adversaries. In Matthew 28, Jesus spoke to His followers, saying: "All authority has been given to Me in heaven and earth. Go therefore and make disciples of all nations, baptizing them in the name of the Father, and the Son, and the Holy Spirit, and teaching them to observe all that I commanded you; and lo, I am with you always, even to the end of the age."

Can any statement be more powerful? Jesus now is depicted as the leader of those who are choosing to join the Kingdom of God. The question that usually would follow is, "Are you on the Lord's side?"

Presenting the saving Grace of God in Jesus Christ as the only viable and acceptable option is customarily a rhetorical statement. This is the assumptive close to a theology that compels the responders to accept God's call on their lives. Can we choose to accept or deny God's plan for ourselves? Do we, in effect, have control over God? Can we dictate whether we stay in God's kingdom by making our own decision to follow Jesus or not? Most Christians would answer a resounding "Yes" to these questions.

In that famous Nicene Creed, does it really mean that no one was saved until this incarnate one came down from heaven? Did God make a mistake by not providing salvation until millions upon millions of Old Testament people had died? What happened to them? What happened to all the people who drowned at the flood or died in the desert during the forty years of wandering?

In answer to these questions, explore with me the following Scripture so that we might discover its eternal truth for all of God's children:

> Now we have received, not the spirit of the world, but the Spirit who is from God, that we might know the things freely given us by God, which things we also speak, not in the words taught by human wisdom, but in those taught by the Spirit, combining spiritual thoughts with spiritual words.... But we have the mind of Christ." (I Cor. 2:12ff.)

Here we have the heart and soul of Christocentric truth. For me, the most exciting feature of the "mind of Christ" is it's eternal watchdog feature, which examines us on our spiritual journey through our Alpha-Omega eternity. The Lord has determined that we shall never be free to compromise the truth, and that we always shall have His truth to scrutinize our every decision, whether appropriate or inappropriate. In Psalm 139:1ff, the child of God recognizes that the Lord searches him, scrutinizes him, and slays the lies that he [and we] seem more than willing to adopt as our gods.

In exploring this truth, we need to visualize that as God's children we are placed in God's kingdom and are unable to escape. We have not been expelled from this kingdom for our sins, and thus do not need to confess our sins before gaining readmission back into the heavenly realms of God. We are not free persons burdened with the responsibility of deciding for God's kingdom or for some alternative. We are free to live within the kingdom of God.

When I introduce this truth to the inmates, I equate it with the fences surrounding them. There are double twelve-foot fences with razor wire at both the top and bottom and with a six foot concrete rat wall below the ground. Within these confines, we are able to experience our prescribed world, with the ever-present Christ-God supervising our activity. Sometimes I discover that this is such a new concept that it is difficult to accept, because the men spend great periods of their prison time thinking that life does not begin until they leave the prison confines.

In the world in which we and these inmates have been placed, we have accepted that upon our physical death we shall enter a new perfect state with God. Unfortunately, this lie or illusion has been a distraction to our living effectively in the Alpha-Omega eternity of God. This world is bounded only by the decision of God at the time of our creation. If we were willing to believe the truth, we could decide that heavenly living, while wearing our physical bodies, is the optimum choice.

As God's children, we have spiritual truth so immense that the most spiritual of God's children has barely begun to explore it. Our minds have been given an intelligence so great that even Albert Einstein is estimated to have used less than one-tenth of one percent. Our physical universe is so large that the finest scientists can only offer guesses as to its expanse. If you feel claustrophobic in thinking that you are in a closed system, take several "peace of God" tablets and meditate on God's love for you, as He watches over you throughout eternity.

The Christ-God interjects Himself into our activity only when we sin by failing to honor the truth implanted in us by the Creator-God. Then we are in need of judgment by the Christ-God. (You should be mindful that delineations or indications of partitioning of God is only for our understanding.) Jesus Christ did declare that we all have violated the truth and underestimated the greatness of God; hence, we need the Christ-God to judge us and declare us guilty of our violations of the truth.

After we have been declared guilty by Christ, we are then sentenced by Christ. The sentence of Adam and Eve is declared in Genesis 3:24:

So He drove the man [and woman] out; and at the east of the garden of Eden He stationed the cherubim and the flaming sword which turned in every direction, to guard the way to the tree of life.

While we understand the sword to be a cutting instrument and an instrument used for killing, the Christ-God cuts us cleanly from our sin and violations of truth, and kills us from ever being able to participate in that Eden again. Consequently, we are dead to our past opportunities, and now we are given new fields in which to labor and live.

Be assured, there is a price to be paid for our transgressions. We sometimes realize our sin and desire to pay that price; however, we have nothing of our own to satisfy the debt. Consequently, Christ-God had to pay the debt, and this is illustrated for us in the physical with Christ dying on the cross.

Dying and being born to live again are opposite sides of the same coin. Unless we die to yesterday, we cannot be born to today. As Christians, we affirm that Christ is the ground of our hope and the promise of our deliverance from sin and death. It is important that we believe this truth; however, more important than our believing and affirming it is the truth that after dying, we are born by the grace of God.

Paul reminds us of this truth in Ephesians 2:4-10:

> But God, being rich in mercy, because of His great love with which He loved us, even when we were dead in our transgressions, made us alive together with Christ [by grace you have been saved], and raised us up with Him, and seated us with Him in the heavenly places, in Christ Jesus, in order that in the ages to come He might show the surpassing riches of His grace in kindness toward us in Jesus Christ. For by grace you have been saved through faith; and that not of yourselves, it is the gift of God; not as a result of works, that No one should boast. For we are His workmanship, created in Christ Jesus for good works, which God prepared beforehand, that we should walk in them.

Therefore, we are always children of God because God has chosen to be our Father-creator. As such, we are not needed by God to prevent His being usurped by other Gods. God is perfection beyond our comprehension, and anything we do neither increases nor decreases this truth. We do not make God happier because we honor Him nor unhappier because we do not observe His commands.

The wrath or judgment of God is a blessing to us that eternally expresses God's care and protection. Our contemptuous attitudes and behaviors toward God only prove God's truth is permanent. The reward of God's care and protection is a gift given to us prior to our creation. God has given us enough truth to live perfectly and expects us to do so. However, God being God, He has covered for our presumptuous insolence with the Christ-God, whom we would so crucify.

God's plan for us, His creation, always has been to "Be fruitful and multiply, and fill the earth, and subdue it; and rule over...every living thing that moves on the earth" (Genesis 1:28). When Adam and Eve were moved on into another section of eternity, they were to continue living this command. Adam was to cultivate among thorns and thistles while shedding the sweat from his brow. Eve was to bear children while experiencing the pain of childbirth. Gone were the hours of work without suffering. These persons now became challenged by their new surroundings, while attempting to understand their relationship with God.

God has told us all that "we should have life and have it abundantly." This is God's purpose for creating us. He has given us the liberty and freedom to discover what abundant living means. Three of the elements by which we define abundant living Christocentrically are eternal life, eternal knowledge, and eternal faith.

Eternal Life

The first of the three elements of life is eternal life. We are ordained by God to live eternally. In John 3:16-21, we are given specific instructions for living our lives. God commands us to live our eternal lives now. As spiritual beings, we are to search our souls and discover the excitement of living that God has breathed into us.

To successfully understand this gift of eternal life, we need to move beyond the limited physical definition we identify with life and into the new paradigm of our spiritual living. The difficulty for many of us in doing this results from our fear of observing ourselves as spiritual beings, with or without physical bodies. So long we have identified ourselves by our physical characteristics that we forget the physical body is only the suit that we wear in order to be seen while we live in this limited area called the Earth.

As we learn to focus, we will improve our ability to make spiritual decisions without allowing our mental or physical conditions to compromise them. In the eternal spiritual world, we always are perfectly whole, purposefully occupied as God commands, and fully supplied with all our needs.

As spiritual Adams and Eves, we always are happy doing the Lord's work, eating the Lord's food, and enjoying the Lord's heavenly eternity. We are living in wonderful peace with God. We know only perfect love, truth, peace, and complete relationship with God and all the animals. All the animals are so kind to each other that the lions do indeed lie down with the lambs. Walking with snakes, alligators, puppies, and all the other exciting animals in this garden is such fun.

It has taken years of contemplation to enable me to understand this truth. With this understanding, I have found that when I experience demanding problems I am able to confront them with less physical or mental stress. The more aware I am of my spiritual being, the more I find that I am able to control my mental and physical being.

This became more apparent to me about three years ago, after I had had numerous operations on my back and neck for a disease of my spinal cord and vertebrae. I found that I was losing the feeling in my left leg and was having constant and severe pain in my back. When I went to see my neurosurgeon, he told me that I could have an electronic implant placed in my back to override some of the pain, but I very likely would soon lose the use of my leg and become wheelchair-bound.

Janie and I prayed and talked about this problem, and God gave us another solution. In September 2001, we were watching the evening news and fell in love with a puppy that was being offered for adoption by the animal shelter in Urbana, Illinois. The thought hit both of us at the same time that we should adopt that dog and he would help me walk my leg and back troubles away.

We got up very early the next day and drove to Urbana, arriving there over two hours before the shelter opened. We wanted to be the very first ones there for that dog. We took that beautiful Border Collie-Black Labrador puppy into our hearts and family, brought him home, and named him MacDuff. We go walking with MacDuff several times each day, and I now have very little pain in my leg and only minor numbness in my toes. MacDuff believes that he is the one who is getting the opportunity to walk, but in reality he is providing the healing I need. Recently, I was examined, and the doctor reported that my condition had essentially been arrested.

I believe that professing the spiritual truth that I am a whole creation of God can dominate and control my mental and physical being. I do not assume that you will quickly adopt this basic truth; however, I urge you to allow yourself to breathe in the truth of your perfect wholeness, which is provided by Christ.

Reflecting back on my early life, I now understand how God has been nudging me to make proper decisions throughout all of my life. As a child, I often would be permitted to go to my Grandmother Button's house. She and my grandfather had suffered through the Depression, as had my parents and our entire family. This included losing their small farm and living on beans, rice, and other commodities that were earned by working for the township or county. Although their plight was not dissimilar to millions of other Americans reduced to the poverty level by the Depression, my grandmother always seemed to me to have perfect peace in her life. She was a great joy to be around.

I loved to listen to her tell stories of when she was a little girl. She also told me about life on the farm, including the time she saved my father, as a four-year-old, from a wild mother sow. It happened at farrowing time. My father wanted to play with the piglets, so he crawled into their pen. Soon a sow noticed him and headed toward him. He began screaming as the sow started mauling him. My grandmother ran across the yard, jumped the fence, and rescued him. He escaped with only bruises and cuts to show for his curiosity. My grandmother told me that she sprouted a few gray hairs from the ordeal, but was too thankful to God to discipline my father.

She later told me that perfect peace, to her, was explained in Marguerite Rnokey-Hall's poem, "Set My Hands upon the Plow."

Set my hands upon the plough
My feet upon the sod:
Turn my face towards the east,
And praised be to God!

Every year the rains do fall,
The seeds they stir and spring:
Every year the spreading trees
Shelter birds that spring

From the shelter of your heart,
Brother drive out sin,
Let the little birds of faith
Come and nest therein.

God has made His sun to shine
On both you and me;
God, who took away my eyes,
That my soul might see!

Grandmother Button is still in my heart. I thank God for her and for her gift of sharing perfect peace with all whom she met. My mother recognized this grace and peace in my grandmother. I have heard my mother tell of the wonderful friendship and love they shared throughout the forty-two years that they knew each other. My mother often joked that while she dearly loved my father, she was determined to keep her mother-in-law forever as a friend. My grandmother participated with God in her eternal life while living in her beautiful physical body. She lives among us today dressed in her spiritual body. She "is sown a natural body, [she] is raised a spiritual body"(I Cor. 15:44). What a wonderful blessing this is!

Throughout my life, God has blessed me with multitudes of persons, both in the physical and in the spiritual. I love studying Scriptures in order to be awakened to the realization of this blessing. As I have done so, I have experienced more and more happiness. I desire to continue to climb the mountains of life with God and enjoy the good news of His peace and joy for all of us.

In Isaiah 52:7-12, God speaks to me and, I hope, to you of this truth:

How lovely on the mountains
Are the feet of him who brings good news,
Who announces peace
And brings good news of happiness
Who announces salvation,
And says to Zion, 'Your God reigns!'
Listen! Your watchmen lift up their voices,
They shout joyfully together;
For they will see with their own eyes
For the Lord has comforted His people,
That all the ends of the earth may see
The salvation of our God.
For the Lord will go before you,
And the God of Israel will be your rear guard.

Jonathan Swift spoke of this wonderful opportunity that God gives to us, when he wrote, "Spilled in the earth are all the joys of eternal life, and vision is the art of seeing things invisible." This art of seeing that we are living in the eternal is beautifully illustrated for us in Mark 5:41.

Here Jesus has been brought to the home of an official who believes that his daughter has died. Jesus approaches the child and says to her, "Talitha Kum." Jesus is speaking to the spirit of the child, which knows only the life given to it by God at creation. This is God calling forth the Alpha-Omega life of His child.

This calling-forth is the identical truth that I experienced through the ministry of Loyal Morris Thompson, the pastor whom God sent to Kewanee during twelve of the most important formative years of my life. He wrote both prose and poetry to share the spiritual truth he lived. In his poem "The Wild Bird Song," we can perceive this spiritual truth.

The wild bird song I love to hear
Where untried trails in silence meet
It breathes a strain of mystic cheer
That stays my restless feet.

The eventide oft brings to me
The whisper of a still small voice;
It breathes a reverent ecstasy
That bids my heart rejoice.

And I by faith do somehow know
Where birdsong and still voice blend
In mystic harmony - and lo,
He's present - My ETERNAL FRIEND.

This is eternal life. Jesus restores Talitha as He restores us from any sense of incompleteness. For all His children, He demonstrates God's perfection ministered eternally.

Can we see this eternal truth as Peter saw it when he looked into Jesus' eyes, stood up in the boat, stepped out on the water, and walked toward Jesus? Can we see this truth as Moses saw it when he was with God on the top of Mount Sinai, being handed the Ten Commandments of truth, which were and are for all God's people? Can we see what Noah saw as he closed the doors on the Ark, obediently setting his face toward a new realm of his eternal living with God?

Can we see this eternal truth as the framers of the Declaration of Independence saw it as they wrote, "all men [and women] are created equal, that they are endowed by their Creator with certain unalienable Rights, that among these are Life, Liberty, and the pursuit of Happiness..."? They pledged their lives, their personal wealth, and their honor to the new world that only God could see. They were unafraid of life that would include physical death. They knew that men's hearts were very frail and that the road would be very steep and lonely, but they had seen a wonderful God who set aside the impossible and made it possible. Their truth went beyond cold, icy rivers to cross, beyond blood spurting from the chests of brave men and women, and beyond treason from former blood-brothers, to the new eternal life that had now been shown them in their souls.

Can we see this eternal truth as the great visionary, Dr. Martin Luther

King Jr. saw it when he was presented with his "Mountaintop Experience"? This experience began while he was in the shoe department of Blumstein's Department Store in Harlem in 1958, signing autographs on his new book, "Stride Toward Freedom."

Mrs. Izola Curry approached him, asked if he were Martin Luther King, and then drew a sharp object from her dress. She thrust it into his chest and beat him with her fists while babbling incoherently. When the doctor removed the Japanese letter opener from his chest, he told Dr. King that it had made a cross over his heart. The next time Coretta, Dr. King's wife, heard him speak, he said, "Coretta, this woman needs help. She is not responsible for the violence. Don't prosecute; get her healed."

As Dr. King recovered, he decided to accept an invitation from the Gandhi Peace Foundation to visit India. During his month-long epic journey, he realized a peace and solitude that would continue for the rest of his life. Dr. King was on the mountain that God created for him. Dr. King came to realize and to understand that Gandhi had a nonviolent mission to replace the government of India. This mission had grown out of the teaching of Thoreau on the purpose of civil disobedience toward an unjust government.

This experience served as the opportunity for Dr. King to clearly see God's eternal truth and it's meaning for him. This dynamic lesson meant that Martin Luther King Jr. was to love his enemies even while they might be beating him to death. Dr. King said, "There comes a time when a moral man can't obey a law which his conscience tells him is unjust. And the important thing is that when he does that, he willingly accepts the penalty." He also said, "I will be obedient to a higher law."

He sought only to be included in the existing world as an equal member of it and to achieve this goal through nonviolent means. This walk through the eternal truth of God was, for Dr. King, historic and monumental. However, he soon found that his followers did not easily learn this form of living, nor was it appreciated by his enemies.

Unfortunately, we who think we understand and appreciate Dr. King's truth now leave it to history rather than continue to practice it on a worldwide scale. Instead, we have placed that time and those monumental lessons in a historical time capsule rather than seeing them as active directions for our living.

Can we see this eternal truth as Malcolm X saw it at Mecca when God showed him that all men are God's children? Malcolm then realized that his fight was against evil manifested in the world regardless of who the perpetrator may be. This great man set an example by educating himself while in prison and committing himself to a pure life of truth and love, which has become an inspiration of God's living truth to many.

All of these persons have defined living as responding to God moment by moment. This was done by breathing in the fragrance of life that God inspired in them and opening up to God and the world with total peace and divine commitment. They were like flowers that open up for all to see the beauty, to inhale the fragrance, and, then, to offer themselves for others to use.

We see this same beauty as we look into a baby's face and eyes. We can observe the incredibly intimate relationship between the baby and God. At this moment, the baby is the closest to the pure soul relationship with God that we are given an opportunity to witness. This moment is so sacred that we often fail to see it and only partake of the beautiful glow of the child. This glow is the child's spirit overflowing the small physical body with which it now is to be identified.

Some teach that the baby is like a blank tablet and that, as adults, our responsibility is to fill its little vacant mind with all it will need for living. This teaching is irresponsible and damaging to the new parents. Treating the baby as a blank tablet denigrates this beautiful gift from God. If we assist this child in celebrating its eternal life, we will have participated in a blessed opportunity to enjoy our own eternal lives. William Butler Yeats said that educating the child is not the filling of a pail, but the lighting of a fire.

Many of us are profoundly ignorant of the participation the Creator God has in the birth process. God places each soul/spirit in the womb of the mother at the moment of conception. If conception by normal physical intercourse is difficult or impossible for a couple and they question how their relationship with God could be involved, the couple can experience much distress.

The couple often needs to understand that they are in a mystery that may only be revealed to them as they continue to open themselves to God's purpose and will. It is possible that the couple's physical constraints may lead them to examine other opportunities such as adoption. Sharing with God in His purposeful placing of His children with us can be one of the most complicated of life's lessons and can be very difficult to accept and understand.

The biblical story of the relationship of Abraham and Sarah effectively illustrates this truth. Sarah was barren, so she offered Hagar to stand in her place. Hagar bore a son, Ishmael. When God told Sarah that she was to conceive Isaac in her old age, she had difficulty understanding how she could live with Hagar in the household because of the constant reminder that

Abraham had fathered Ishmael. This story is so convoluted that most rational people need to admit that God certainly can make living in this Alpha-Omega eternity both interesting and challenging.

Does this mean that for those who have difficulty or even the impossibility of conception because of physical problems are deemed by God as inadequate? Of course not. One need only examine the wonderful strides that specialists have made in the field of infertility to discover the desire of God that we have life. I believe that we will more and more understand that conception can include countless ways of receiving the blessings of life that God has prepared for us. Many couples have found their child in a crib in China or Romania or the Philippines or in a hospital in the United States. Has God not prepared that baby for this mother and father?

This life truth is shared with us in II Peter 1:2ff, "Grace and peace be yours in abundance through the knowledge of God and of Jesus our Lord. His divine power has given us everything we need for life and godliness through our knowledge of him who called us by his own glory and goodness…" If we choose to go to our soul/spirits, we can discover this abundance.

One day many years ago, The Rev. F. B. Meyer, of Christ Church, London, recognized Hudson Taylor, the missionary, in his congregation. He invited Mr. Taylor to give a brief address to the congregation. With characteristic modesty the missionary said: "I am not prepared to give an address, but if you are interested I shall be glad to tell you what has been the motto of my life. It is Mark 11:22, 'Have faith in God.' There have been times in my life, especially during my sojourn in China, when it seemed as though everything was against me and I could not go on, but on such occasions, I have trusted God all the more, and He has never failed me. I have often been foolish in my judgments, and fickle in my conduct, but whenever I have trusted God, He has given me the victory."

The word "courage" comes from the Latin *cor*, meaning "heart." Courage is not a matter of the head, but of the heart; not of understanding, but of the feeling; it is not a matter of theory, but practice. One may know all the theory of courage perfectly and still be a coward. Love prompts courage, love of a dear one, love of one's church, love of one's home, love of Christ. (Taken from a newspaper article by Archer Wallace, circa. 1944).

In summary, we need to examine ourselves to see if we believe that we "are the salt of the earth" (Matthew 5:13); that "we have eternal life" (John 3:36); that we "have passed from death into life" (John 5:24); that "we are in Christ and loved by the Father" (John 17:23); that we "are children of God"

(Romans 8:16); that we "are holy temples of God" (I Corinthians 3:17). Do we believe these truths for ourselves and will we live them?

How many of us are still caught in "sweet-bye-and-bye" thinking or in pipe-dream theology? Can we only believe if we have no critical challenges to face and to defeat? Maybe the hardest part of Christocentric truth is believing that we are living to profess God's truth in us. This is the only thing that God cannot do for us. We must decide if this day we will live; we must decide if this day we will "pick up our bed and walk."

Eternal Knowledge

The second element in the Christocentric truth of God's gift of living and dying is knowledge. We are given all knowledge to perfectly live in the eternity in which we are placed. We are told that this knowledge is given to us in Deuteronomy 29:29b, "the things revealed belong to us and to our sons forever, that we may observe all the words of this law." God wants us to declare that we are free of any lack. God wants us to know that we are capable of solving any and all challenges that we experience.

God, in creating us, predisposed us to correctly implement His directions and commands. As I first considered this initial contact between ourselves and God as being totally God determined, I remembered that we were operating within God's imaging power and that this is the first step in His plan for our emergence into His eternity. In Psalms 23:1ff, we are reminded again that we dwell in God's pasture and are directed as to how we shall live. I find, in this truth, more comfort than anger at being under God's control. If you are not comfortable with the idea that God manipulates His creation, consider that we are created as God imaged us and eternally manages us. It is this management of us by God that constantly challenges us to hit a hole in one in life.

Recently, we were traveling in England and became friends with a Welshman named David Ladd. He was very witty, quite engaging, and very scholarly. One afternoon in our travels around that beautiful country filled with wonderful cathedrals, David related the following story of the great Mozart to me:

In 1782, Mozart composed the opera "Seraglio." One of his great admirers was the emperor of the Hapsburg dynasty of Austria-Hungary. After seeing the opera with Mozart, he leaned over to Mozart and said, "It seems a little long to me." At which the maestro replied, "I can't understand that. It has all the notes that belong in it."

70

This speaks volumes to me, for I interpret Mozart as affirming that God had given him the knowledge of the complete opera, even if others did not always understand. Do we understand or appreciate the gift of knowledge that God has given us and others?

When I reflect on some of the great masters of art, music, and science, and observe their gifts of creative expression, I rejoice that God knows just the correct notes to place in all His creation. In the same way, we are gifted by God with the ability to do His will and the responsibility to "pick up our cross and follow" His direction.

Fanny Crosby, blind throughout her life, wrote over eight thousand great inspirational poems. Many of these have been made into hymns through which we can find God's truth.

Her poem "All the Way My Savior Leads Me," is one of these.

All the way my Savior leads me; All the way my savior leads me;
What have I to ask beside? Cheers each winding path I tread,
Can I doubt His tender mercy Gives me grace for every trial,
Who through life has been my guide? Feeds me with the living bread.

Heavenly peace, divinest comfort, Though my weary steps may falter,
Here by faith in Him to dwell! And my soul a-thirst may be,
For I know what-e'er befall me, Gushing from the rock before me,
Jesus doeth all things well; Lo! a spring of joy I see.

All the way my savior leads me; When my spirit, clothed immortal,
Oh, the fullness of His love! Wings its flight to realms of day,
Perfect rest to me is promised, This my song thro' endless ages:
In my Father's house above, Jesus led me all the way.

I love this hymn because in it Fanny tells me that God's leadership is good, comforting, and tender. I recognize that I do need God to guide me. I bow before God and receive His leadership. I thank God for giving Fanny the knowledge of and the ability to express this truth.

Also consider the story of George Frederic Handel. Until composing "The Messiah," he considered himself a failure in life. Yet God had other plans for him. First, he received a commission from a Dublin charity to compose a piece of music for a benefit concert. Second, a wealthy friend, Charles Jennings, presented him with a libretto based exclusively on Bible texts.

With the text in hand, Handel went into a feverish work mode. For three weeks, beginning August 22, 1741, he confined himself to his small house on Brook Street in London. From early morning into the night, he rarely left his music paper, ink, and pens. A friend who visited at that time reported having seen Handel weeping with intense emotion. Later, as Handel related the compositional experience, he quoted St. Paul's words: "Whether I was in the body or out of my body when I wrote it, I do not know."

At one point a servant came into Handel's room to deliver a tray of food. He reported having seen a wild expression on his employer's eyes; a weeping Handel refused the food and exclaimed, "I did think I did see all Heaven before me, and the Great God Himself." He had just completed what has become the most performed choral movement in history, the "Hallelujah Chorus."

After six days of this incredibly concentrated work, Handel had completed Part 1. Part 2 took him nine more days, and Part 3 another six. In two more days the orchestration was completed, and the masterpiece called "The Messiah" was finished. In the unbelievably brief span of twenty-four days, Handel had filled 260 pages of manuscript. One of Handel's many biographers, Sir Newman Flowe, gave this insight: "Considering the immensity of the work, and the short time involved, it will remain, perhaps forever, the greatest feat in the whole history of music composition."

The creative process that was given to Handel by God also has been given to us, and we can observe it in our world today. All of this has been programmed in us by the Great Creator God. I challenge you not only to contemplate these magnificent productions, but to bleed the blood of the creative intellect that God has birthed in you. If God has given you a life puzzle that seems impossible to decipher, He also has planted the solution in you.

As a child, I grew up in Kewanee, Illinois, in what today would be called a poor working-class neighborhood. The forty or fifty kids in our neighborhood provided ample opportunity for our parents to mete out discipline on a regular basis.

We all played together during the week. Our fathers went to work, usually in the local factories, and our mothers were housewives, when that word was not pejorative. We went to school every day during the school year except when we were too ill. Fooling our mothers was not easy as they had all the remedies for every malady. Expectations were always very high regarding our behavior in the neighborhood, in school, and especially in church.

While living in that neighborhood, I had a dream or vision that has impacted my life ever since. In this dream Jesus was standing at the foot of my bed. He took me by the hand and led me out into the world. I was directed by Him to go up to doors and knock on them and quietly tell those who answered of Jesus' love. We did this for quite an extended time. Jesus explained that He wanted me to do this throughout my life.

As a nine-year-old child, I was deeply impressed by this and told my parents about it. My story became common knowledge among our family and in our church community. If any one doubted its veracity, no one told me, and no one said I was crazy or told me to forget it. Quite the opposite, everyone seemed to deeply respect its validity. In fact, no one considered it other than authentic until 1984, when I asked my Methodist bishop and his cabinet of district superintendents for permission to accept the correctional chaplaincy position at Jacksonville Correctional Center. They immediately sent me to a psychiatrist for evaluation.

As I got older, I sought out virtually every opportunity to do church work. When I graduated from high school, I enrolled in college aiming to be a minister. During this period of my life, I sowed some wild oats, which expanded my worldly knowledge but probably couldn't be used in college for academic credit.

In 1958, after several of these adventures, I returned home to get a new perspective and direction for my life. Within a week, I met the woman who was to become my wife. I was taken by her beauty, her intelligence, her patience, and her love and kindness. Two months later, I knelt at her feet as she sat on a boulder under a harvest moon on the top of Starved Rock overlooking the Illinois River. Jane Harlan and Phil Button were married December 27, 1958, and moved into their first home in Bloomington, Illinois. God certainly knows when to give gifts, and I am able to say that I didn't pass this gift up nor will I ever do anything except thank God for Janie, my lovely bride of more than forty-three years.

Within two weeks, I was appointed pastor of two small churches in north-central Illinois. While Jane was finishing her last year of college, she became pregnant with the first of our four children. After her graduation, I enrolled in college in preparation for seminary.

Among the many stretching experiences that Jane and I have had was one that has most changed and impacted our lives. It occurred in seminary while I was in a chaplaincy program. As part of our training we were confronted with problems that helped us to examine our reactions to stress. The purpose was to train us to be pastoral care-givers and not pastoral manipulators. This helped us to critically examine our relationships with our patients, our mates, our families, our fellow seminarians, and our congregations, whether they be in a hospital, a mental hospital, a prison, or in a church community.

When I explained this training to Jane, my lovely wife, she brought to my attention that I had left out my family, and especially her, in most of my decisions and actions. She helped me become aware that I was too much wrapped up in myself and needed to begin to listen for a change. God had given great knowledge to Jane, which woke me up, and we began to explore the meaning of our relationship.

Often, we need to experience the siren call of another person in order for us to awaken to our implanted knowledge. The difficulty we often experience in accepting this awakening is that our ego gets in the way of the new learning. I have often expressed an "attitude" when alerted to a problem that I might be unusually sensitive about and resistant to face. I do not know if any other male has a problem recognizing a driving issue such as speeding or adhering to the rule of stopping at stop signs. However, I have often experienced a loud scream, "STOP!" Getting my ego out of the way has been a goal of mine, and this has led us to so many more years of blessed peace and love. I daily thank God for the incredible gift of love that He gave Jane to take this "leap of faith."

Since leaving seminary, I have enjoyed much of the ministry, including preaching, counseling, and especially the friendships of the pastorate. What I haven't appreciated are the incongruous religious faith statements that theologians have determined to be the only acceptable truth and the political game-playing that is necessary to be considered a success in the ministry. I have been disturbed to see the terrible guilt that these theologies have heaped upon us, His children, and the destruction in congregations and pastors' families as the political games are played.

Out of these concerns, I have dedicated myself to intensely investigate accepted theologies and affirmations in order to test their validity in light of the truth as implanted in us and contained in the Bible. From this search, I have been blessed with the knowledge of Christocentric truth, which supersedes all religious theologies. Also, I have experienced a general hunger among laity and clergy for an opportunity to express unity across normally forbidding religious moats, filled with the serpents of anger and hostility.

In December 1984, I was appointed to the position of chaplain in Jacksonville Correctional Center. I began to experience personally the destruction that was taking place in men's lives. Thus, I began a serious journey to discover if all this confusion was necessary, and if there was anything I could do, even on so small a scale as a prison chaplain, to assist men in resolving their feelings of estrangement and rejection.

Immediately upon reporting to my district superintendent and my bishop that I had been offered and had accepted the responsibilities as chaplain at the prison, I experienced this same rejection. Prior to this happening, I had counseled with both that I was interested in filling this position were it to be offered to me. Both had encouraged me to pursue the opportunity; however, on the very day I notified them that I had received the appointment and wanted their continued support, I was harshly reprimanded.

At that time, I was serving the oldest Methodist congregation in Illinois, which also was in Jacksonville. I told the bishop and the district superintendent that I would continue to serve as pastor of the church until a replacement could be found. Instead, they immediately severed me from my duties to this wonderful congregation, which numbered about 600 members. I protested, requesting that I at least be allowed to officiate at one last service in order to announce to the congregation my appointment as prison chaplain. This I was allowed to do after much heated conversation.

I was then ordered to attend a meeting of the Methodist Church Cabinet, which included the bishop and seven or eight district superintendents. At this meeting, they quizzed me extensively, suggesting that I needed psychiatric help. I consented to an evaluation with a psychiatrist and a psychologist after one of the district superintendents posed a rhetorical question, "You do believe that possibly everyone at some time or other might need or appreciate some counseling. Don't you? Why, even I can think of times when I could have been so helped." Not wanting to appear insolent, I replied, "Yes, I believe that counseling can be of help to many in such need." Upon that basis it was decided that I should go at the Cabinet's expense to see about this testing.

Once the testing was concluded, I was invited to return to the psychiatrist's office for the results. I admit that I was a bit apprehensive about this session, consequently, I asked my wife to accompany me. The psychiatrist and psychologist were reluctant to allow Jane to attend, stating, "The information is confidential and some of it might just be very disturbing." I told them that we had been married for twenty-seven years and that my wife knew everything about me there was to know." She stayed!

The first mistake these two "professionals" did was to give me a written copy of the evaluation. (I am referring to it as I write this seventeen years later.) In it, they reported that I had Axis II personality problems; that I had personality dysfunctions and lived in a fantasy world; that I was trapped in intense conflict while withdrawing from personal relationships; that I lacked self-esteem and anticipated pain and disillusionment; that my occasional attempts at autonomy had led me to seek supportive institutionalization which I resented; that I was self-delusional and passive aggressive; that I was unable to sustain stable loving relationships; and that I was an alcoholic and a fugitive from the law. If I were to consent to treatment, any possible success would involve long-term and intense interpersonal counseling.

Soon after this interview, the bishop contacted me and informed me that I had "just left the ministry by accepting the chaplaincy position at Jacksonville Correctional Center." Consequently, I was being severed from the Methodist Church and without endorsement as a correctional chaplain. This being a condition of my employment, I then sought and received endorsement with another national chaplaincy endorsing body.

This has caused me a great amount of anguish and pain because I had been a Methodist all my life. I believed that I had been called into the ministry through a vision at nine years of age. I experienced this "vision" being validated over the next thirty years as I studied for and received my local preacher's license, accepted appointments, and served as pastor. The first appointment came within two weeks after marrying Jane. While completing my college degree, I received my second appointment.

Then I applied to and was accepted by Wesley Theological Seminary located in Washington, D.C., in order to pursue my theological training. I also was appointed to a three-church charge in and near Norrisville, Maryland (this was a 600-plus member charge that had always been served by a fully ordained pastor). These congregations, plus my seminary education, further assisted me in growing into the pastor/minister that God had called me to be.

I received my first ordination during the summer following completion of my first year in seminary. At the end of my second year in seminary, I enrolled in and successfully completed chaplaincy training under the supervision of James Hall. This training was an intense and confronting experience that trained one to be both an effective chaplain and pastor.

We were a select group of twelve men who had scrutinized our every word and action. This was done by tape recording our patient visits, chapel meditations, and interviews. Using these recordings, we were critiqued in order to eradicate any inappropriate or self-serving language. The end result was to ensure that we were effective listeners and healthy counselors.

When I graduated from this program, my wife and I assessed our situation and found that we were in an emergency situation financially. This was 1966. By this time we had four children, and the salary of $3600 a year from the churches did not provide enough means to care for our needs. Some members in one of my congregations told me about a teaching position in special-education that was available. I applied for and received this assignment while continuing my pastoral responsibilities to my assigned churches.

At the end of that year, we returned to Illinois, where I accepted a pastorate that allowed me to obtain my master's degree in special education. I then took a teaching position as a special education teacher, leaving the pastoral ministry for about five years. At the end of that time, I sought and was appointed to a small, yet vital United Methodist church in eastern Illinois. I served there as pastor for over five years before being appointed to the Jacksonville Centenary United Methodist Church as directing minister.

While at Centenary, the political pressure of the bishop and his cabinet effectively placed a demarcation in my ministry. I had to decide whether I would continue as a Methodist minister or surrender my ties and become a correctional chaplain. Consequently, with the knowledge that God had given me, the support of my wife, and the success that I had experienced as a pastor-counselor, I decided to proceed with the correctional chaplaincy and the challenges it held for me. I knew that God had given me the knowledge to serve His will even without the support of the Methodist church and clergy.

It took me about fifteen minutes to find that prison was where I belonged. The inmates were kind and loving. It was obvious to me that God was in their midst and I was the one who was blessed to be there. The first time that I told the inmates that they were all children of God because God is the only Creator and Savior, I was not prepared for their reaction. It was like a building had been lifted off their chests and they could breathe again.

About a year ago, I preached a sermon focused on Jesus calling the children to him in order to demonstrate God's love and affection for each and every child. My purpose was to encourage the men to accept the child in themselves as God does. I hoped the men would then believe that, as children of God, they can serve God and their fellow brothers and sisters rather than fighting for a place in the kingdom of God.

Randall was one of the many inmates who was deeply affected by this sermon. His life has so dramatically changed that after that as he worked on the serving line in dietary, men begin to smile and exchange "God bless you" greetings. He led many men to closer relationships with their families, and he recited that sermon to me so many times that I can now recite his version by heart. He told me that for him to now know that he is a child of God is the most wonderful present that he ever received.

Hilario, who has such a wonderful smile and a glow about his face, wrote a beautiful note to me following our study of the eighth chapter of Romans. In the note he said, "Now for the first time in my life I know that I am a child of God. This knowledge makes me happier than I have ever been in my life. Religion has always been such an unhappy experience for me that I had almost given up on searching anymore. Now, there is such a thrill running throughout my body that I want to shout for joy all the time. However, I would get in trouble, so I just smile and people smile back at me. Sometimes they ask why I am so happy, and I tell them that I am a child of God and so are they. This often either leads us into a conversation or they want to argue. I will talk with them, but I will not argue. I enjoy the peace I have in my heart, and I look forward to returning to my family and being a good father and husband.

These kinds of reactions from ones who now accept the knowledge that they are children of God make me want to shout, but I just smile and thank God for this same knowledge.

Eternal Faith

The third element in God's Christocentric life gift is faith. Faith is the drive in each of us to arise from the mat and participate in the get-up-and-go of living. It is the spark that makes a crocus begin to sprout in the late winter. It is truth manifested into action.

In Matthew 15:22ff, Jesus is hassled by a Canaanite woman who has come from her home to seek out this man whom she KNOWS will heal her sick daughter. She is willing to suffer any humiliation for her goal to be realized. She is willing even to die for this sick child. She will not cease her pilgrimage until her goal is realized.

She cries out in a loud, disturbing voice, "Have mercy on me, O Lord, Son of David; my daughter is cruelly demon-possessed." Here we have the white blood cells of life rushing to the scene of the accident and screaming, "Do something! Do something! Do anything to stop the bleeding!"

This obviously is causing great consternation on the part of all those gathered around Jesus to calmly hear Him tell his wonderful stories and to encourage them to believe. Yet, here is this uncouth and uninvited foreigner disturbing this tranquil gathering. Something must be done to end this intrusion.

The disciples attempt to get rid of her, but only cause her to scream all the more. They now begin to look like bodyguards and bullies. This begins to affect the crowd, so the disciples call on Jesus to get rid of her.

Jesus looks at her and His response is difficult for us to understand in our world of politeness; however, if we listen to His statement to her, we begin to perceive his motives. "It is not good to take the children's bread and throw it to the dogs," he says. Here he is keeping the crowd of self-righteous Jews at bay while ministering to her, because they are persons without a cause and she is a woman who will not be denied.

She responds appropriately, "Yes, Lord; but even the dogs feed on the crumbs which fall from their master's table." Does she care that she is being humiliated; does she care if she is ridiculed? Obviously not, for her answer reflects her focus. She wants her daughter healed from this terrible demon, and Jesus is the one to do it. She will endure all manner of discomfort to achieve her daughter's healing.

This faith component of our eternal living is placed in us to make us function. Paul identifies this implanted gift in II Corinthians 2:13 and again in 7:5. In the first reference, he wrote: "I had no rest for my spirit, not finding Titus my brother...But thanks be to God, who always leads us in His triumph in Christ, and manifests through us the sweet aroma of the knowledge of Him in every place. For we are a fragrance of Christ to God."

I can just imagine the wonderful relief that came over the crowd when Jesus answered the Canaanite woman, "O woman, your faith is great; be it done for you as you wish." Jesus had taken an impossible situation and turned it into a sweet aroma for all to enjoy. In 7:5ff, Paul likewise identifies this conflict and resolution: "For even when we came into Macedonia our flesh had no rest, but we were afflicted on every side: conflicts without, fears within. But God, who comforts the depressed, comforted us by the coming of Titus."

How wonderful when we are led by the faith God has placed in us to seek until we find our questions answered and our problems solved. The end result of Christ's coming in our midst appears not to give us new duties and responsibilities, but to allow us to express the longing we have to repair old breaches of our duties and responsibilities.

Faith implanted in us causes us to be restless until this breach has been resolved. The resulting healing is refreshing and, as Paul relates, "To those who are perishing: to the one an aroma from death to death, to the other an aroma from life to life." If this is as clear as mud to you at this point, I ask you to be patient for I will return to this issue in the next chapter.

For us to understand this faith drive, we need to define it as a verb. It is eternal life in action, movement that cannot be curtailed until completeness is restored. It is best understood when viewed in its raw, uncompromised, sacrificial state.

Hannah Senesch lived in Hungary during World War II when, as a girl of eighteen, she felt called to aid the Jewish refugees. She volunteered to train as a parachutist. She eventually persuaded her officers to permit her to parachute into enemy territory, since the enemy would not expect a mere girl to drop from the skies. Convinced that she indeed was willing to undertake the mission, they relented. However, when she was dropped from the airplane she landed in Yugoslavia, hopelessly tangled in parachute cords. She was captured, imprisoned, and eventually executed. In her cell she wrote words that swept Europe. They became a password in every Ghetto, sung by every refugee in Palestine,

> Blessed is the match that is consumed in kindling flame;
> Blessed is the flame that burns within my heart;
> Blessed is the heart with strength to stop its beating for honors sake;
> Blessed is the match that is consumed in kindling flame!

"Are Ye Able? Said the Master" is and always will be a question posed to anyone brave enough to feel the suffering imposed upon one such as Hannah. "Lord, We are Able" will be the answer given by only those who feel the blood flowing from Hannah's body, who feel the anguish of those imprisoned to die in the death camps, and who feel the dedication to cross the burning desert.

Faith has judgment as a part of its definition because we have to face the hard realities of the present that confront us. We can take a pass on becoming involved or we can believe the moment is our call to live. That moment is usually as difficult to understand for the one exposing himself as it is for those affected.

A friend of mine is a prime case of faith in action. Herb is a man in his middle to late forties, yet he has a remarkable freedom continually to exhibit faith activities. Recently, he sat down with me and related portions of his life story. He said that he grew up in a small community with a population that was essentially socio-economically homogeneous. When he was eight or nine, a very poor family moved into this town. It was obvious by their clothes, or lack thereof, and the house that they occupied that poor was an elevating term to describe their circumstances.

From the very beginning they were shunned and humiliated. People would cross the street to avoid meeting or being near them. Herb remembers that one day when he was in fourth grade, his best friend was especially abusive to the ten year old girl as she arrived at school. He was calling her name to other children in a way that made one feel as though she did not exist. The other children also began to join in with this abuse. Finally, Herb ran over to this young girl and stood between her and the others and shouted, "Leave her alone, stop calling her names or I'll beat you all up!"

He remembers that at that moment the whole world stopped. No longer did he have any friends. No longer was he the great guy to be with in school or anyplace else. That night when he got home, he told his parents about the action he had taken. His mother and father made a decision to make friends with the Burnetts.

Herb's mother baked a pie, and they went to the Burnetts' house and introduced themselves. The Burnetts were invited to their home. Good clothes were quietly given to the family. Herb says that even today, he will occasionally see the now grown woman, who is a teacher in a town near his home. She still thanks him for that eventful day.

Herb calls himself weird because while others seem to value acceptance and security, he has an ability to be able to live liberated. This does not mean that he is loose in his relationships. He is a husband of twenty-three years, a father of two very loving and gifted children, a leader in his church, and a successful businessman. He is able to leave all but the first two commitments when God opens new doors.

I have watched Herb express his faith, and the best word I can use to describe him is "peace." He is at peace with himself, his family, and the world in which he lives. He has eaten steak one day and beans from a can the next, but in either case he is always stepping out to help others. He has a happiness that is infectious. Having spent a fortnight with him on a choir tour recently in Great Britain, I witnessed his faith and leadership in difficult situations.

Herb has recently turned over a very successful business of several hundred employees to other leadership to start anew in an endeavor currently known only to God. This business was one he started from scratch about five years ago, and with his leadership it flourished while hiring persons who were accepted on the basis of their desire to work regardless of their background. The pay scale was always higher than others in this field were paying.

Herb closed our meeting stressing that other people must think he is crazy or weird, but he said: "I believe that God takes care of all of us and His only requirement for us is to live like children of God and to love His fellow children. Our two children have been told from a very early age that they belong to God and their mother and I are only given this brief opportunity to act as their parents."

Do you believe Herb is a little short of a load or is he right on in his beliefs?

In Chapter 9 of First Samuel, Saul is asked by his father to solve a problem. The problem involves only going into the desert to find lost donkeys. This doesn't appear to be a very important task for a man as young and handsome as Saul. Possibly Saul thought the request to be somewhat arcane, yet he honored his father. After a few days of searching fruitlessly, he almost decided to return to his father and tell him that, although the donkeys could not be found, he had returned safely.

Instead, he and his servant decided to search for a seer to ask for insight on the whereabouts of the animals. They were directed to a man named Samuel, who was hurrying to a ceremony. He told Saul that the donkeys had returned home safely and invited him to the ceremony. Samuel seated Saul at the head of the table and proceeded to anoint him king.

Had Saul considered the request of his father too unimportant or had he turned back, he probably would not have met Samuel and become king. Saul's persistence and bravery in facing the desert of his life at that time ended in his being anointed.

Songwriter Mark Hayes wrote a hymn reflecting this spirit of dedication called "Walking in the Spirit."

> Now Moses saw the spirit of God
> He came down from the mountain with a smile on his face,
> For Moses saw the glory of God.
> Now Joshua heard the spirit of God,
> He blew his trumpet at Jericho
> And the walls came atumblin' down
>
> Now David knew the spirit,
> David knew the spirit of God.
> When he played his harp so melodiously
> The evil spirits left old Saul.

Now Daniel knew the spirit of God.
Even down in the lions' den Daniel believed,
And the lions' mouths were shut.

Do you have the spirit?
Do you have it?
It's a good, good feeling way down in your soul,
When you're walking in the spirit of God."

Yes, we are faced with the question of whether we are alive by Christ. Do we have the Spirit, for "God sent His Son into the world to judge the world," that we might "have eternal life?" Do you have eternal life? Do you HAVE eternal life? Do YOU have eternal life?

CHAPTER 4
Freedom and Liberty

Freedom and liberty are the gifts God gave to us as we were formed by His hands at our creation. They became useful and critically important to us when He moved us from the restricted confines of the Garden west of Eden to the farm east of Eden. In our new location we would be held responsible for the choices we would need to make in order to survive the rigors of our independence. No longer could we walk aimlessly in the Garden and suffer no consequences. The liberty that we were given requires us to relate to the laws of God. We continue to be challenged as to our willingness to keep God's precepts.

This myth of God's moving us from the Garden to the farm east of Eden symbolizes our entry into the mature phase of God's creation. This is Christocentric truth because, as SABBATH PEOPLE, we now are living in God's kingdom, but with additional responsibilities. We will use the freedom and liberty we have been given to live and explore the entire kingdom in which God has placed us. We also have been provided with God's grace to explore this kingdom without the limitations that failure would impose.

Without God's grace, we have no freedom or liberty. Without God's grace we would be continually in jeopardy with no option to fail, because if we did we would be culled from the flock. The freedom we now have is not the result of our sins as Adams and Eves. Nor has it originated in the evil that has resulted from these transgressions. It is God's gift of grace that permits us to live effectively without recrimination. Paul explains it in Romans 5:15-17:

But the free gift is not like the transgression. For if by the transgression of the one the many died, much more did the grace of God and the gift by the grace of the one Man, Jesus Christ, abound to the many. And the gift is not like that which came through the one who sinned; for on the one hand the judgment arose from the one transgression resulting in condemnation, but on the other hand the free gift arose from many transgressions resulting in justification. For if by the transgression of the one, death reigned through the one, much more those who receive the abundance of grace and the gift of righteousness will reign in the life through the one, Jesus Christ.

The gift of justification has always been present with us since creation. However, prior to our corporate sin, which is identified as arising in us as Adams and Eves, we were unaware of its truth. Nor did we even need to be aware that freedom, liberty, or justification were gifts implanted in us by God. Whether we ever are able to completely integrate into our spiritual psyche the need for the primal sin, we at least need to relate to the gifts given to us by God. These gifts afford us the spiritual tools to live perfectly in our new habitat.

Although we seldom will appreciate it, death also is a gift of God. Death is analogous to justification of our sins by Jesus Christ. Without death we would discover that living outside of Eden would be impossible. Death is the removal of the barnacles that we accumulate by misusing our liberty. It is Christ-God's judgment that scrapes these sin sores from our spiritual bodies. Consequently, we would never be able to discover life with its ever-changing challenges and discouragements without death and the judgment that follows.

Life, then, can be defined simply as having the freedom and liberty to do anything we want to do. The only caveat is that it is our responsibility to live honoring God and our fellow humankind. We have the freedom to decide what honoring God and our fellow brothers and sisters means and the method that we will choose to accomplish these goals.

We can and will try everything, sometimes succeeding, often failing. Does it make a difference whether we succeed or fail? Only we can answer that question as we proceed through our life experiences. Some failures will be especially hard when we see our loved ones suffer, or when we see babies killed for any reason, or when we are in the midst of terrorism that has begun because of lies told and believed.

We shall be completely baffled at the time of a disaster when thousands may die in a moment. We shall be exalted when we all celebrate the fulfillment of God's purpose for us, but in all of our eternity, we shall learn that Sabbath living is a journey. Men shall fruitlessly forecast the end of the journey because they believe that living is an end with rewards and punishments. This illusion or lie will gather many adherents. Every postulation will prove incorrect; yet, they will not flag in their efforts. They or others of like ilk will analyze the stars, the tragic and catastrophic state of the human condition, or the resources that appear sufficient to terminate humankind and declare that the end is at hand.

We also shall learn that every other person whom God has created has an effect upon us. This makes the mystery of liberty and freedom all the more difficult to comprehend. Our choices can result in joy, peace, happiness, and love, or in judgment, pain, and suffering.

We sometimes will believe that we understand this mystery. However, most of the time we will make decisions with little or no sense of direction. We may often only hope that we will better understand what God was "thinking" when He granted us the privilege of determining how we are to live in this eternal time, with this freedom and liberty.

As we examine this truth, we shall discover the dynamic and joyous opportunities available to us in interacting with one another and God. We shall also almost certainly discover extreme pain and sorrow. Freedom and liberty are evasive and serpentine gifts. Just the moment we believe we are exercising them correctly, they will slip away, and we will appear as lost babies in the sea of life.

Christocentric truth commands us to believe that it was God's will that we be compelled to use our liberty to make choices. Choices are the most precious gift we have been given by God, yet they are the most terrifying. We experience the first taste of Sabbath living when, as Eves and Adams, we must make decisions.

Consider the pressure that now is placed upon us. We would like to stay in our familiar surroundings. After all, even if the present conditions in which we are living are somewhat intolerable, we have learned to survive and to deal with them. Maybe the next situation will be worse. We may question why a just god would place these burdens upon us. We may even lose focus and begin to view our physical and spiritual decisions as having little or no effect upon each other.

Choices! Choices! Choices! I often find it easier to understand the ramifications of our freedom and liberty when I examine individuals and their relationships. In Jeremiah Chapter 1, God is talking to Jeremiah, reminding him of a conversation they had prior to Jeremiah's appearing in the flesh. God reminds Jeremiah that he was created to be a prophet to the nations. He also assures Jeremiah that protection will be his and elaborates on Jeremiah's specific duties.

If you believe that this interaction might actually have occurred, then might a similar conversation have taken place between you and God or between me and God? Do you think that God has spiritual intercourse with us before we are placed on this earth? Many find it difficult to acknowledge that God can have relationship with His creation before we take up residence here on earth.

Back in the early nineteen-eighties my wife, Janie, and I attended some seminars at the Crystal Cathedral in Anaheim, California. One of the lecturers was Dr. Robert Merkle. He had a unique way of presenting biblical truth by telling the stories in simple language, using modern cliches to provide dynamic emphasis. I have attempted to use some of his phrases and concepts in telling the following story of what might have been an interchange between God and me.

On one beautifully perfect day that was just like all the other beautifully perfect days in eternity, I was walking with God in the garden of eternity. As we walked along, God was doing the talking as He usually did, and I was listening as was my custom. God asked me a question that surprised me because God had never asked me a question before. I have to admit that others had told me that they had heard of God asking questions. God asked me, "What do you see?"

I told Him that I see everything and all is perfect.

He then looked down and again asked me, "What do you see?"

I replied, "I see where I have never been before and what I have never seen before. What am I seeing?"

God looked at me and said, "What you see is a part of eternity not meant for you."

I looked again and replied," I want to go there!"

He said, "If you go there you will not live as you do now, instead, you will be required to take part in an experiment to determine if souls can work together when they do not have sight to see me all the time. In fact, many who go there believe that they are lost and refuse to help each other accomplish the experiment."

Everything God said convinced me more and more that I wanted to go on this mission, however God did everything He could do to discourage me. He told me that living there would be like living on a spaceship. I admit that I had little understanding of what God was telling me.

Many songs and conversations later I asked God, "What if I went for just a little while and then came back?"

God said, "You cannot come back if you go there." He said that many leave this place and spend most of their lives trying to get back here instead of making a new life there. God said, "These souls are causing a lot of trouble for all those who are trying to make the space experiment work."

When God told me that this place would no longer be my home, that it would exist for me no longer, and that I should not expect to see it again because I would be on an eternal journey throughout the universe, I admit that I was both terrified and awestruck.

God told me that if I go from here I will need to find a space suit to wear. He then explained that to get a spacesuit, I would need to locate a factory that manufactures them and rent a spacesuit for nine months. He said that going through this factory would be much like being on an assembly line or like being in a long tube. As I progressed through it, various attachments would be added that I would need when I emerged at the shipping dock. He urged me not to go searching for that spacesuit, but told me how much He loved me and would always love me even if I decided to go. He then seemed to be gone because I couldn't see Him any more. I guess I already was looking for that manufacturing plant.

When I found it, I didn't think it was so bad. It was just like before. All of my needs were being met and I was very comfortable, except that God appeared to me and asked me why I had decided to go on this mission through eternity. I felt bad and replied, "I heard that others had done it and it didn't turn out so bad. Maybe the devil made me do it." God appeared to leave me and I wondered where my reply to God's question had come from, for I had never ever heard that word before.

Well, everything seemed to go along pretty well except this manufacturing plant began to get awfully small because of the parts being added and expanded. Before I could put in a complaint, terrible things started to happen and the next thing I knew two big claws were grabbing at me and pulling at my spacesuit. I thought they were trying to take it away from me, so I pulled back as hard as I could. The next thing I knew was that I had been completely evicted from my manufacturing plant and someone was beating on my spacesuit. That was when I let out a shout that even scared me; however, I looked around and they were obviously very proud of themselves. They were screaming, laughing, and hitting their hands together over their heads, a gesture which I later learned meant to "high five." I wanted only to get back in that manufacturing plant and head for home.

They did wash my suit off in something warm and placed me in a warm place. After all this fighting, I had something shoved into my upper hole. I started to work with this new spacesuit and got some pretty good tasting liquid. I was too tired to do any more fighting so I just put it to rest for a while. When I awoke, they were messing with something which I heard them call a diaper. They were down smelling at something and I used part of my spacesuit to shoot them in the face. Boy, did they jump, but this still didn't convince them to send me back where I was before they arrived.

This whole business went on for quite a while, and I almost forgot about those days when I went walking with God in the Garden until it happened. I was nine years old at the time when Jesus stood at the foot of my bed and then, taking me by the hand, led me out into the world, where He guided me and trained me in the work for which I was to give my life.

I never have been able to deny that experience and I am now in my mid-sixties. Since then, I have been blessed with how this blessing can assist others in realizing their God-given talents and truth.

God has placed our souls in these spacesuits so that we have the opportunity to relate our physical bodies to our spiritual beings. In doing this, God already knows we will become confused and sell out to the physical, as does the writer of Psalm 17. God also is fully aware that we have chosen a walk in the park of eternity with its many pathways; hence, we shall need an eternal sword to cut us free from the vines when we become entangled. The eternal sword, of course, is the Christ-God.

In truth, I have not always appreciated the gifts of God or the call of Christ; however, whether I am in the flesh or out of it, I always am in God. I can and have failed to live the truth and have experienced unhappiness, anger, fear, and other equally unpleasant results to myself and also to my family. I have been continually blessed with God's forgiveness, my bride's ever-fulfilling love and devotion, my family's equally blessed love, and many new opportunities from God to serve Him. Today, I desire to realize as many of God's opportunities to serve and love Him and His children as I am blessed to receive.

Jeremiah is faced with the same set of choices in his conversation with God. We, like Jeremiah, need not be afraid of the journey on which we are now embarked. We will experience information that appears to be deceiving, contradictory, and/or false; however, we will always be provided with all the solutions if we choose to use them. We also can convolute the information and guidance we receive from God, deceiving ourselves and others.

Well, who can step in to help? None other than the Christ. How does He help? He is "despised and forsaken of men" because we believe we can handle it ourselves. He is the sacrificial lamb and is "smitten of God." He is sent by God into the war as a lamb to the slaughter. In Matthew 25, Jesus explains in a parable how He becomes our sin-cleansing agent whenever we choose to sin and violate God's purpose for us. I am retelling this story in my own words.

The parable is about a young couple who plan to get married. The bride enlists the assistance of ten of her friends, who are also yet to get married. She needs their help in preparing her for the wedding and to assist is carrying out the ritual of proving to the father of the groom that her hymen is intact until it is breached in the wedding tent outside his house. The groom also gets together ten of his buddies, who will help him prepare for the service and assist in any other needs that arise.

On the day of the wedding, the ceremony comes off just fine until the bride and groom go into the tent to consummate the marriage. It seems that five of the young ladies that are waiting have a distinctly different opinion of the groom than the other five. These ladies only brought a small amount of oil in their lamps, while the others brought along an extra liter of oil. The first five must have known this man when he was younger and as someone who didn't take long for these things when they went to the drive-in. The other ladies knew him to be quite a man at these love-ins. Consequently, five ran out of oil and had to walk back to town to buy more oil from the 7-11.

While they were gone, the bride and groom emerged from the tent and signaled the remaining young ladies to come and get the bed clothes to take and show daddy. The bride and groom knew that there would not be any blood from the broken hymen on the bedclothes, so they had the ten best men go out and get a lamb, kill it, and bring it's blood to pour over the sheets. When this was done, the sheets were taken to the father to confirm that the marriage was official and the bride and groom were pure. Then the gates to the house were shut and all danced and celebrated for days over the new pure couple being married.

In this parable, Jesus is telling us that He is the slaughtered lamb that perfects our imperfections. The lamb of God has been prepared for the slaughter. His blood has washed over our sins. We are now perfect. Did we make ourselves perfect? No! Christ died for our transgressions. That is why Christ is the sword, on the cutting edge of sin, sacrificing Himself that we be constantly perfected. Do we remain in the room that we have just destroyed and that Christ has just cleansed? No! We are moved by God to a new opportunity to be tested to see if our "Want to" is now aligned with God's requirements for us.

In Matthew 25, this young couple needs the groom's father's blessing and approval in order to seal the marriage. Without that approval there would be no marriage and no banquet. The bride would be sent away in disgrace. The father knew the freedom this couple had and the liberties they had taken. He provided his lamb for the blood they needed as their entrance into the mansion where the rejoicing would take place. The father already knew their needs and met these needs before the youngsters knew they were in jeopardy. God is our only remedy, as He has born our afflictions.

God is the perfecter who redeems us in our marriage ceremonies and throughout our marriages. I believe He brings us together, encourages us, inspires us, and supports us in our relationships. If we visualize every meeting as a sacred moment, we may possibly honor God's incursions into our lives as having greater holiness.

Another young couple met in 1994. It was a one-in-a-million chance that they ever would meet. They even said that God must have brought them together. They soon discovered that they shared common values and interests. After a brief courting and engagement period, they got married in a beautiful ceremony attended by family and friends.

Everyone was very happy for the couple. The bride and groom could only see a perfect life before them. She was an elementary school teacher, and he was a commercial pilot with a major airline. They looked forward to having children and living the great American dream. They decided that apartment living was not for them and bought a house that was under construction.

They were able to choose the kitchen cabinets, the wall coverings, and the other things that will make this house their dream home. When it was finished, they moved in. Bill carried Susie across the threshold and life began in this their piece of Eden. They were the ideal couple. Susie was petite, always happy, and very beautiful. Bill was tall, very handsome, and was well on his way to an excellent future as an officer.

Soon, Susie announced to Bill that she was pregnant. They both seemed so very, very happy that God had blessed them in this wonderful way. This happiness hit a snag when Susie began to have complications. She was placed in the hospital in order to save baby Ben from coming way too soon.

While lying on her back and being very bored, Susie began to write notes to God in an effort to lay her pains and suffering out to one she felt would understand. She began:

Dear Lord,

I have now been pregnant and in bed for thirty weeks, and forty of those days have been in the hospital. Each day Ben gets healthier. I had a sonogram, and he was so beautiful! Bill went shopping for clothes and of course bought a lot of things that I thought were not practical. We had a fight. He doesn't even like me anymore. I know that he comes only because he feels obligated. How cruel can he be for telling me, his pregnant wife, he doesn't love me anymore? Maybe baby and I would be better off without him. He's not supportive anyway. What do You think I should do, Lord? Am I being too hard on Bill?

With our freedom, we can make choices for all the wrong reasons. Is this what Susie and Bill have done? Were their courtship, marriage, house-buying, and pregnancy all for the wrong reasons? Was Bill looking at Susie and marrying her for her beauty and for sex with her? Was Susie marrying for stability and for babies? Is the trouble that they are having because of their different priorities? Is Bill now viewing Susie as damaged property? Is he asking himself why he was so stupid for making this mistake by getting married in the first place? As he visits Susie in the hospital, is he kicking himself for choosing Susie to be his wife? Before marriage, he could date and "bed down" any broad he wanted. Now he is tied to this witch who keeps telling him what to do and who is crying all the time when he visits her. After all, marriage and having babies was supposed to be an easy affair. Why should it include Susie being laid up in the hospital?

Possibly God was interjecting some opportunities in this couple's marriage in order for them to use their freedom. Did He now want this couple to realize that they, too, were Adam and Eve? Eve must bear the pain of childbirth. Adam was required to live among the rocks and thistles of life. Could Bill and Susie comprehend their relationship to God as a sacred event?

In Genesis 25-34, we have a similar problem presented to us. Jacob, as a young lad, was pampered and spoiled by his mother, Rebekah. Since she favored Jacob over his older brother, Esau, she conspired against her husband, Isaac. First, she helped Jacob acquire Esau's birthright. Then she helped Jacob steal Esau's blessing from his father.

This deeply angered Esau. Esau vowed to kill Jacob, so Jacob was sent to live with his mother's brother, Laban. While on the journey, Jacob had a dream that convinced him God was with him. Consequently, when Jacob awoke, he built an altar and vowed that he would tithe if God would watch over him and eventually return him to his father's house.

Upon arriving at Laban's, Jacob fell in love with the first person he met. She happened to be Laban's daughter, Rachel. Jacob pledged to work for Laban for seven years in exchange for marrying Rachel. However, Laban slipped Leah into the bargain, and Jacob had to work an additional seven years for Rachel.

Then, Jacob found out that Rachel could not bear him children because God had closed her womb. This resulted in Jacob having numerous children with Leah. The story gets racier because Jacob started having children with Rachel's handmaiden at Rachel's insistence. Then, Leah gave her handmaiden to Jacob to have more children in order to out-produce Rachel.

Here we quickly can realize that these marriages and the children who follow are for all the wrong reasons. There appears to be little or no positive relationship between Jacob and his wives, Leah and Rachel. The relationship between Jacob and his Uncle Laban is very convoluted. Everything that happens seems to arise out of selfishness and greed.

Can we live our lives with no regard to God's ordinances? Why do we conceive that God's burning indignation will not bring us to our spiritual knees? God cannot be mocked. We cannot create God for our own personal use, nor can we use this clown of our creation for justifying our insolent behavior.

Is this a course of spiritual behavior that Susie and Bill are pursuing? Could they possibly be unaware of how they are misusing their freedom? Perhaps God is forcing this couple to recognize His presence. They refuse to stop and look at what they are doing to themselves and to Ben in relationship to God's purpose for them.

In her next letter to God, four days later, Susie recognized that the road to the destruction of their marriage was far more serious than she previously was aware. She writes:

Dear God,

I think that Bill and I are in grave danger of losing each other. Last night, I tried to call him for an hour, but the line was busy. When I asked him who he was talking to, he told me it was Helen. But, when I talked to Helen, she said they had not talked for a week. I accused Bill of lying, and he got pissed off that I didn't trust him. He sounds like someone who's guilty to me. He told me that he didn't like me as a person anymore. I told him not to come back to see me. O, God, what are we to do?

Two days later, she wrote again:

Dear God,
Thank you, my loving Father, for Your help with Ben. He is such a dear
baby! I long to see him. I know that You are taking care of all of us. I am so
happy that I got to go home yesterday. I haven't been having many
contractions.

In her last letter, Susie wrote:

Dear God,
Bill and I need help, but we cannot talk to each other any more. Bill has
been writing and calling someone he met when he was on a lay-over in South
Carolina. I found her name and phone number in his wallet and a note she
had written to him calling him sweetie and writing XXXOOO on the
note....This is supposed to be such a happy time. I feel so sick and miserable!
Lord, I know that You must have so much to do, but we do need Your help!

Baby Ben was born just a few weeks short of full term and things got better
for a short while. Bill and Susie had fewer and fewer fights, but Bill still
would not talk with Susie about his feelings. About a year went by, and Bill
began treating Susie cruelly again. This time Susie just wanted Bill to go
away so that Ben would not hear the angry insults, the yelling, and the
slamming of doors.

This was followed by some brief periods of quiet and peace. Susie even
believed that maybe Bill had matured, and now their marriage would go
smoothly. She decided to forgive Bill for that woman by convincing herself
that she was at fault for nagging Bill so much.

One peaceful period resulted in Susie becoming pregnant again. The
pregnancy went smoothly this time, and after nine months a brother for Ben
arrived. Susie took a leave of absence from her teaching position in order to
provide the mothering the boys needed.

The loss of her income soon became a financial issue and was elevated to
a boiling point at the end of every month. Consequently, Susie capitulated
and returned to her chosen profession, while leaving the two boys with a
sitter. This change did nothing for the relationship between Susie and Bill.

Finally, she sued for divorce. After months of counseling and
negotiations, the divorce was finalized. On that eventful day, Susie decided

to drive to her family home to celebrate with some friends. On the way back, she had a one-car accident and died that night.

After Susie's death, Bill found her letters to God. He read about her feelings and the trials that their experiences had caused her. He realized the part that he had played in this troubled marriage. After a few days he decided to write a letter of his own to God.

Father God,

Today, I decided to write a letter to You. It has been five months since Susie died. I know that she is with You. I am so sorry for my behavior. I ask both You and Susie for forgiveness. I have looked back at all her letters to You and have realized what a terrible husband I had been. I realize that the divorce was unnecessary in order for us to put aside our differences and to start over again. Unfortunately, Susie and I will never have that chance.

God, what I hope for in the future (and I pray for) is that You will give me another chance to love another and to take those vows again that I did not take seriously. After Susie's death, I have fully realized all the mistakes that I had made and the biggest one was pushing You out of my life.

God, I now realize that You do things to bring us back into the fold. Susie was trying very hard to point this out to me, but I wouldn't listen. I will and have learned from my mistakes. I will pass those lessons on to Ben and Matthew. I will continue to grow in Your word. I believe that You are giving me another chance. You have sent a very special person into our lives (Missy Lyons). God, I will continue to pray and seek Your guidance in all things I do.

We do not know if Bill even now realizes what "praying and seeking God's guidance" means or if he will keep the commitment that he made in that one letter. We do know that God will keep His part of the bargain as he lives in the Sabbath.

In Psalm 51, David wrote much the same message to God, confessing his grievous sins and asking God for forgiveness. David also desired that the joy of his salvation be restored in his life. This did not happen until the death of the son born from his sin.

David, this couple, and millions like them are free to choose marriage or divorce, free to love or hate, free to experience joy or sadness. We can only hope and pray that in their choosing, they will learn to make better choices. Unfortunately, Bill and Susie didn't learn from their errors, and their marriage ended in divorce.

See what God did by placing us in the Sabbath to live? We can now live and experience life for all the wrong reasons and for all the correct reasons. In both we shall experience death. Death to our decisions of yesterdays. Death to opportunities not taken. Death to relationships, to roads not traveled, to hopes not realized. Why did God decide that we should travel this sorrowful road? Yet, would we give back our freedom, our liberty, our chance to live? Can we possibly live and not have to experience failure?

Jacob's story did not end with his return to his father's homeland. It continued and in each of its additional experiences, Jacob was exposed to opportunity upon opportunity to serve and honor God. The first thing that happened was a meeting between Jacob and Esau. Jacob desired to make peace and gave Esau many sheep, goats and cattle. Esau told Jacob the gift was unnecessary.

Esau's response to the gift helps us to understand that Jacob's sin harmed Jacob and not Esau. Jacob's violations of God's commandments eroded his relationship with his family and with God. This was a relationship that only God's judgment, followed by His forgiveness, could satisfy. God pronounced death upon Jacob's sin. However, God required Jacob to honor the knowledge of His forgiveness. Jacob shed the ill-gotten gains of his sin and built a pillar to God. God cleansed Jacob and named him Israel because God chose him to multiply the nations.

Should Jacob or any of us anticipate anything other than additional tests in our lives? Obviously, anyone who has lived long enough to experience joy and pain in their life will expect some of each in the future. Life is, in itself, a test.

In Christocentric truth, we look to these tests for opportunities to serve God. This may often involve our choosing to suffer the ignorance of others who believe that it is foolish to serve a God who calls us to feed the hungry or clothe the naked. Can we live and not be aware of the needs of others? In Peter 2:18-19, we are summoned to investigate whether we are using our freedom to corrupt others or to serve the purposes of God. We are free to condemn those who are blind and living unrighteous lives; however, we are worse than the most evil of the unrighteous if we use our liberty for condemnation.

How much better we are when we identify the gifts we have been given as coming from God and dedicate our lives to exercising God's will. This decision involves our choosing to accept the posture of humility. We must look to the will of God for our guidance rather than consider the gain that we may personally receive.

One of the groups that has beautifully demonstrated this focus on God's will to the men in prison over the past fifteen years is the Mennonites. They have passed out Bible study booklets, which the men can individually complete and send to graders. The graders review the answers and then respond to the men with notations indicating how well the work has been done. I have had men bring these graded books to me in order that I might see what the grader has written. Without fail, the man has been given encouragement and support in his search for God's truth. The glow on the face of the inmate from the grader's comments is a reward that will provide the energy for his next test in serving God.

Helen Keller wrote, "The infinite wonders of the universe are revealed to us in exact measure as we are capable of receiving them. The keenness of our vision depends not on how much we can see, but on how much we feel." We, as God's children, have been plunged into the Sabbath world by the God who believes in and loves us. It is a world of unknown demands. We now can expect to receive experiences that will both startle and amaze us. Helen Keller was a woman who learned to live life in God's light, but only after she died to living life in darkness.

Whether one believes that we might have been able to resist God's enticements to die to the status quo of remaining ignorant, we obviously could not pass on the challenge. God moves us along into the maze of our eternal quest. Then, He hounds us with His presence by continuing to evaluate us in our decisions. In Ezekiel 36, God was very forthright in declaring His reasons for this pressure on us. He announced that we have profaned His holy name, and that we are being transported to new challenges to test if we will declare our allegiance to Him. God is like a blacksmith who places his masterpiece in the hot coals and then removes it to his anvil where he shapes it. We are God's masterpiece.

It is similar to a parent telling a two-year-old child, "Don't touch or you'll get burned." Can you guess what the child will do as soon as the parent turns her back for a minute? The child may not touch the hot object or the child may decide to test the parent's statement for its voracity. The child's decision is probably based more on curiosity or defiance to the parent than on spiritual integrity. How often are we choosing to defy God? What do you do when God forces you to choose whom you will serve?

Paul writes of this same determination in Colossians 1:9ff: For this reason also, since the day we heard of it, we have not ceased to pray for you and ask that you may be filled with the knowledge of His will in all spiritual understanding, so that you may walk in a manner worthy of the Lord....For He delivered us from the domain of darkness, and transferred us to the kingdom of His beloved Son, in whom we have redemption.

Do we believe that we are delivered or do we still imagine that we are in darkness? Do we fight God because we believe that we have been given an unfair slice of eternity?

Remember, God told us that we love the darkness rather than the light. If we are delivered, what does this mean to our present reality? Why do we not feel more relieved? Shouldn't we be happier with the gifts that God has given us?

The writer of Revelation 2:2ff commends us for our deeds, our toil, our perseverance, and our ability to identify and test evil men. However, he condemns us because we are no longer loving God, who is our source of all meaningful life. He calls us to repent of our wanderings because the sword is coming to cleave the lies from us. How can we cease wandering when every time we are questioned as to our choices, we experience judgment? Do we even know how to love God anymore?

God has given us freedom to face new challenges. His desire for us is that we will choose to love Him in the process. If we are given sight, will we return and thank God for our healing? If we are given our "right mind," will we serve God? If we are assisted in crossing the Red Sea, will we praise and serve God? If we have everything taken from us, will we still worship God? How will we live when we have an abundance of blessings? How will we live when we are starving and near death?

In Jeremiah 5, God was disgusted with the Israelites of both Judah and Israel. This hatred came because the Israelites had received their Promised Land, their fancy possessions, their own temple, and yet they worshiped idols. He then decided that it was time to remove all this from them and see if they would reform their way of life. Do you think they did? Did they understand that God was their mainstay? How do we react when we have everything removed from us? Can we worship God when we are sleeping under a cardboard box?

In the sixteenth century, William Kethe wrote a hymn about God's eternal guidance and mercy for us:

> All people that on earth do dwell,
> Sing to the Lord with cheerful voice:
> Him serve with mirth, his praise forth tell;
> Come ye before him and rejoice.

The Lord, ye know, is God indeed;
Without our aid he did us make:
We are his folk, he doth us feed;
And for his sheep he doth us take.

O enter then his gates with praise;
Approach with joy his courts unto;
Praise, laud, and bless his name always,
For it is seemly so to do.

For why, the Lord our God is good;
His mercy is for ever sure;
His truth at all times firmly stood,
And shall from age to age endure

I now realize that God is so very good. I do desire to praise God in my every action and decision, however I too often display my anger too quickly when I am tested. The desire of God to display His power and presence before us is an eternal one. We are purposefully pressured to move in the direction that God wants us to go. God understands that we will come along willingly at times and very begrudgingly on other occasions. We need only to understand and believe that in all these experiences we will be shown God's justice, caring love, and eternal presence.

The justice by which God is righteous in all His actions and the mercy by which He is good or beneficent are infinite. Justice and mercy are also eternally inherent in His divine nature. Whether we completely respond to God's commands or disobey Him with vehement disregard for His truth, we eternally remain within God's presence. One of the best examples of this truth is when Jonah disrespects God's desire to have the people of Nineveh know of His love for them. God remains with Jonah which becomes judgment to him, while the people experience the joy of God's salvation. As they lived in God's Sabbath, why did both Jonah and the people not experience the joy together? Doesn't it often happen to us this same way?

When Jesus walked the Palestine streets and through the towns and cities, why did only a few rejoice? Why did Jesus appear on the scene two thousand years ago? Were we so confused and errant in our choosing that we were destroying God's plan? The answer would seem to be a resounding, "Yes."

However, we again need to remind ourselves that God is perfect and His plan is also. Jesus did not come to fix anything. He came as part of God's plan to remind us of the Sabbath that we were given. He also came to remind us of the responsibilities we must fulfill in this Sabbath. "In Him was life, and the life was the light of men [and women]" (John 1:4). The reminder for us is that Christ-God not only judges, He also forgives and redeems us of our sins and commands that we resume living, "that whoever believes in Him may have eternal life"(John 3:15). Were we given eternal life when we believed, or did we believe because we had been given eternal life? We have eternal life because God loves us. When we believe, we participate in the eternal Sabbath. All our belief and faith are gifts from God to enable us to participate in the eternal Sabbath.

Jesus did come as a man. He experienced the physical joys, sorrows, pains, and life issues that other persons living in His time encountered. He was born in much the same way that other children were born. Under Levitical law, the birthing process and blood would have contaminated the inn. If there were no birthing room available, the mother would be delivered of her child in a stable where clean hay and straw could be used. Neither Mary nor Joseph are shown to be disturbed by this requirement. They did not protest to the officials that Jesus was the Messiah and, consequently, should have been afforded a special place in the inn.

When He was twelve, He remained behind in Jerusalem conversing with the teachers in the temple while His parents were on their way back to Nazareth. When His parents returned to look for Him and found Him, He appeared somewhat astonished that they were annoyed at His absence. He reasoned that they should have known from previous trips to the temple that He held so great an interest in religious matters.

Here we are given a glimpse of the lack of understanding of Mary and Joseph. They had lived with this boy for the twelve years of his physical life and still were unable to comprehend the person with whom they were blessed to live. This failure of insight is further noted when Mary and Jesus' brothers came to request that he return to the construction business. We who have not personally journeyed with Him can take solace in our lack of understanding Jesus as we are called to go and serve.

These brief pictures of Jesus could have been conceived by the disciples in later years; however, they illustrate little or no necessary information to prove Jesus to be the Messiah. In themselves, they are not definitive proof that He was a man. They appear to be only stories that Jesus related to the disciples while reclining at an evening meal. These were interesting events in Jesus' life story that were included in the Bible by the gospel writers.

The confrontation that occurred between Jesus and the devil during the forty days of His wilderness experience indicates that Jesus was a product of His time. He believed in the devil and was a physical person who experienced hunger, thirst, and the attraction of power. Were Jesus only God in the spirit, manifested in the physical for mankind to encounter, these temptations would be unimportant. Jesus would have been an illusion or a magical trick by God, and in the end would prove to be of no value in carrying out God's plan. The human Jesus needed to be there as much as the Christ.

These stories assist us in understanding that Jesus had the freedom to choose to serve the purpose that brought Him into the world. The greatest physical manifestation of Jesus, which has long convinced me that He was human, is briefly related in an example He used to prove a point about repentance. I believe it was unnecessary because His point had already been made and the extreme circumstances surrounding the illustration almost detract from the repentance question.

This illustration is found only in Luke 13:1-5:

> Now on the same occasion there were some people present who reported to Him about the Galileans whose blood Pilate had mingled with their sacrifices. And He answered and said to them, "Do you suppose that these Galileans were greater sinners than all other Galileans, because they suffered this fate? I tell you, no, but, unless you repent, you will all likewise perish. Or do you suppose that those eighteen on whom the tower in Siloam fell and killed them, were worse culprits than all the men who live in Jerusalem? I tell you, no, but unless you repent, you will all likewise perish."

The mixing of the blood of the slaughtered Galileans with sacrifices and the tragic example of the deaths of the eighteen laborers are such extreme examples of suffering and death that they overwhelm the repentance issue. Many persons, both in that era and in our time, believe that good things happen to good people and bad things happen to bad people. The facts, however, do not substantiate this myth.

Since the eighteen men are dead, they cannot repent. Repentance is a conscious physical act. Using this extremely tragic illustration, Jesus is trying to separate these sinners from their illusions and lies. It would be easy, however, to get caught up in the other legitimate issues surrounding these men and their families and miss the point of repentance.

I believe that these men worked for Jesus' construction company, and their being killed on the job that He was contracted to do caused Him great remorse. This grief may have been one of the issues that caused Him to decide at that particular time to go into the wilderness and search out His future responsibilities to God and His fellow humans.

Most people whom I have heard tell their stories of extraordinary life changes recount a dramatic incident that proved the motivation for that radical change. Am I suggesting that Jesus would not have taken up His cross if this tragic accident had not occurred? Of course not. I do believe, however, that we often are prompted to use our freedom to choose to serve God on such occasions.

Christ-God and Jesus-man emerged from that wilderness to "be about His Father's business." That business was no longer building roads, bridges, towns, and towers, but spreading the message that we are saved and are now in our eternal life. What an amazing fact. I am in eternal life and I might not believe it. Yes, you and I are often willing to believe a lie. We do need Christ in the physical to remind us of the eternal truth. "And this is the judgment, that the light is come into the world, and men loved the darkness rather than the light; for their deeds were evil" (John 3:19).

One of Jesus' responsibilities was to announce the truth to us that we are all God's children and are living in His kingdom, which we had been denying. Another was to erase from our minds the belief that we are not in God's care and protection while in this part of our eternity. A third was to convince us that we have immense responsibilities to live out our purposes while living in the physical. If God were only an illusion while appearing as Jesus, we would receive no strength from Jesus telling us that greater works than these we shall do.

In point of fact, we are currently doing more miracle healings in the average hospital today than Jesus did in all His ministry. Of course, He said that he did not come into the world to heal, to feed, or to teach people how to walk on water. He came to demonstrate what we who have faith might do while living in the flesh and what had already been done for us by God.

Finally, I believe that Jesus' appearance announced that God expected us to realize that we were wasting time by refusing to serve God and by expecting God to solve our problems. We always appear to need God's nudge to carry out His purpose. In Ecclesiastes, God's will for us is illustrated as a purposeful test to convince us that we are to be happy in our Sabbath sojourn on Earth.

We are not here to hurt ourselves or others, to obtain God's favor, to prove ourselves the best of God's children, or to make a fool of ourselves. We are placed here by God to use the wisdom, the understanding, the liberty, and the other multitude of gifts God that has given us. We are to love God and use these gifts for the benefit of all our fellow brothers and sisters. To do otherwise is vanity and self-deceit. We should live as though nothing belongs to us and as though we are completely dependant upon God.

In the middle nineteenth century M. F. Maude wrote a hymn that I pray will be an ever-present theme to nourish and to guide us as together we walk the highways of our eternity.

> Thine for ever! God of love,
> Thine for ever! Lord of Life,
> hear us from thy throne above;
> shield us through our earthly strife;
> thine for ever may we be
> thou the Life, the Truth, the Way,
> here and in eternity.
> Guide us to the realms of day.
>
> Thine for ever! O how blest
> Thine for ever! Shepherd keep
> they who find thee their rest!
> Us thy frail and trembling sheep;
> Savior, guardian, heavenly friend,
> safe alone beneath thy care,
> O defend us to the end.
> Let us all thy goodness share.
>
> Thine for ever! Thou our guide,
> All our wants by thee supplied,
> All our sins by thee forgiven,
> Lead us, Lord, from earth to heaven.

Thus, when we Eves and Adams choose to exercise our decision-making powers and decide to take on our yokes of slavery to our lies and deceptions, we are moved by the forgiving power of Christ-God into a new pasture already prepared for us. If our response to God's questioning presence is that this was our own decision, then exercising our freedom may not be viewed by God as a deliberate act of disobedience. We actually may be living according to God's plan, but misunderstanding the program. God will not tolerate our choosing to portray ourselves as victims by blaming others. We always are held accountable for our sins.

We almost universally justify our own disrespect for God's rules by declaring someone else guilty. Why do we not go to the heart of the matter and declare God guilty? After all, didn't God place decision-making in our midst? Didn't God plant all the stars in the heavens? Isn't it God who draws our attention to the issues that we must correctly survey and solve?

Only God knows the reason for placing the enticing fruit in our gardens. Only God can make us desire to chance death rather than stay in the security of the past. Only God can know that choosing to utilize our gifts of freedom and liberty can involve more than sinning and serving.

Our problem with truth and the justice that follows is the confusion between our physical hew-manness and God's eternity of spiritual perfection bestowed upon us at our creation. We attempt to justify our inappropriate responses by forgetting that we are held responsible to control our physical with our spiritual. Paul referred to this confusion in II Corinthians 5:14-21: For the love of Christ controls us, having concluded this, that one died for all, therefore all died; and He died for all, that they who live should no longer live for themselves, but for Him who died and rose again on their behalf.

The knowledge of the love of Christ is implanted in our souls. Our recognition of and allegiance to this knowledge is the tool we are to use to control our physical.

If we could only integrate into our soul/minds that we have all been taken by Christ in God through the door of Justice and made whole even prior to our violation of God's truth, then we could better respond with joy and happiness at being on this eternal journey (see Ephesians 2:1-10). We have so stereotyped God's salvation that we have deluded ourselves in professing that we have taken it hostage.

We are not Christians because we have adopted the Christian faith. We are Christians because we were saved by Christ prior to our creation. Our delusion is formalizing Christianity into a religion unique from Judaism and Islam. In Matthew 5:17, Jesus told us that He did not come "to abolish the Law or the prophets. [He came] not to abolish, but to fulfill." Paul reiterated

Jesus' truth by declaring that our salvation comes not in circumcision or uncircumcision. "What matters is keeping the commandments of God"(I Corinthians 7:19).

The Christocentric truth of Ephesians 2:1ff clarifies that as Christians we can neither institute nor take credit for our receiving salvation into our lives. We need to reevaluate both the variety of choices God has given us and the liberty we have in our response to those choices in order for us to have a more realistic understanding of the response God expects from us when we acknowledge our salvation.

"Make a joyful noise unto God..." (Psalms 66:1) sounds so very simple, yet when the remainder of this Psalm is read and understood, one might pray for a new definition for joyful. We might question our ability to be joyous when God's terrible and awesome power is disciplining us by presenting us with soul-stretching selections. This is the eternal glory of Sabbath living.

Charles Wesley wrote of this attitude of joy for cleansing in the hymn "I Want the Spirit Within":

> I want the Spirit within,
> Of love, and of a healthful mind;
> Of power, to conquer inbred sin;
> Of love, to thee and all mankind;
> Of health, that pain and death defies,
> Most vigorous when the body dies.

I admit that I, too, want these selections that God gives to me not to be painful. I have a hard time in being joyful and thankful when the new paths I am to travel hurt or cause me or those I love distress. I have problems being in the boiling pot and being refined as silver or gold. I also do not cheer when oppressive burdens are on my loins; when men ride over my head; when I am taken through the fire and water. I guess that I really do not enjoy pain.

Why can't God find more quiet and peaceful ways to get me to bow to Him and to serve my fellow brothers and sisters? Isn't there some medication that I can take so that I can praise God when soul surgery is being done? How did Abraham go so calmly up the mountain with Isaac? How did Noah close his ears to the screaming of dying millions? How many buckets of tears did Job fill as he watched his flocks, his cattle, his servants, his children, and his wife die to prove a point?

Why can't we just wake up one morning, realize our lives are on a new road, confess our love for God, and then settle into our new life? I want to be able to say, "I choose you, God," instead of making the wrong choices again and again. I am always amazed at the Canaanites, who easily recognized Jesus and fell down and worshiped Him even though they or their families were suffering. Many times we learn as much from our failures and sins as we do from our successes. Yet, I would prefer never to fail or sin. Would the disciples have learned as much if they had caught a boatload of fish instead of fishing all night and catching nothing? The answer is self-evident. Peter learned a great lesson when Christ came by and directed the disciples to cast their net on the right side of the boat.

Our personal god-plan might dictate that we always do everything perfectly, but God's plan runs much differently. We can look at nature and realize that death is as much a part of the plan as life. However, death to our passions and sins may not arrive immediately upon our first sin.

The lesson of the forest teaches us that we may go for years before we are confronted by the shock of our separation from our transgressions. Unless one dies, new life does not appear. In the Canadian wilderness there grows a species of evergreen called the Jack Pine, which reaches its best development north and west of Lake Superior. There are also Jack Pine forests found in New England and the northern Great Lakes states. The Jack Pine, as well as its close neighbor the Lodge Pine, are known for their serotinus or late-opening cones. Some remain fixed to the tree so long that the tree limbs even grow around them. They do not deteriorate nor germinate for many years. In fact, they stay intact with their seeds protected until burned by a forest fire. The intense crown fire must pass and the temperature be reduced to 140 degrees before the seeds will open and germinate in the ashes of the former parent trees.

When I look at one of these fabulous structures, I reject my immature musings and bow to their majesty. My friend L. M. Thompson wrote of them:

> He dwelt among his mountains–
> Tall peaks that pierced the sky–
> He seemed so unassuming
> You would almost pass him by.
>
> Until in conversation
> His spirit did impart
> Such gracious hospitality
> You walked into his heart.

The tall peaks' stately splendor
Were but a nameless goal
Beside the alpine grandeur–
The mountains of his soul.

Aren't we so loved by God that He wills us to climb the highest mountains, to swim the widest oceans, to sail into the highest heavens, and to reach the farthest planets? Can we be so selfish as to refuse to oblige God and thus to suffer even physical death so our children can climb even higher? Dying physically really is not a sacrifice when we realize that living spiritually with God is so wonderful.

Didn't the adult Israelites die in the desert or wilderness and only their children cross the Jordan into the Promised Land? I lament that the parents were too selfish to reach the Promised Land. We are birthed in the ashes of our forefathers and foremothers. We also are required to die to yesterday in order to be born to live today. This is the exact truth God brings to us in Isaiah 61:11. In our dying to past lies, deceit, and evil, God brings us forth in righteousness and praise.

Paul knew of this suffering and of his need to rejoice. He said:

> I therein do rejoice, yea, and will rejoice. For I know that this shall turn to my salvation through your prayer, and the supply of the Spirit of Jesus Christ, According to my earnest expectation and my hope, that in nothing I shall be ashamed, but that with all boldness, as always, so now also Christ shall be magnified in my body, whether it be by life, or by death (Phillipians 1:19-20).

Paul's understanding of the freedom of choice and his participation in it is almost beyond our ability to fathom. In Paul's thirty-one years of ministry, he spent almost fifteen years in some sort of confinement, from house arrest to the most heinous dungeon. Yet, he explained his choice in serving God so simply that even we cannot miss its meaning for us. In Galatians 61ff, Paul writes the formula for our service to God and each other:

> Brethren, if a man be overtaken in a fault, ye which are spiritual, restore such a one in the spirit of meekness; considering

thyself, lest thou also be tempted. Bear ye one another's burdens, and so fulfil the law of Christ.... Let every man prove his own work, and then shall he have rejoicing in himself alone, and not in another. For every man shall bear his own burden.

This scripture beautifully explains the myth of the liberty of choice offered to Eve and Adam. It includes the following parts: first, the excitement of being blessed by God with the liberty of choice; second, correctly or incorrectly choosing; third, restoration; and fourth, choosing the new liberty offered by God. We, as Adams and Eves, experience this freedom and liberty throughout our eternity with God, and we need to recognize its blessings.

Jesus Christ used most of His ministry to explain these gifts of freedom and liberty given to us by the Eternal God and Father of us all. Jesus told us we must become as little children. Most of us find this suggestion a little repulsive since we secretly believe that little children need so much care and personal attention. However, this is not what Jesus meant by His statement. He meant that we are to accept His truth with the openness, enthusiasm, and innocence that children have. If we accept God at face value, then we can enjoy our new opportunity to be participants and not slaves in God's Kingdom. To accept at face value God's direction and guidance for us means to live in the spiritual even though we occupy a physical body.

Remember Paul's direction to the brethren in Galatians 6 when he addressed only those who are spiritual? You and I must tear off all our physical coverings to understand the living in which we are to participate. I will try to explain how to do this and how we can identify others who are living spiritually.

If we move to a mirror we will see flesh. Flesh is only the covering over what is underneath, and the bones, muscle, fat, and organs under the skin are facilitators for our souls to interact with each other. We can prove this by making a phone call to another person who has never met us. That person will make judgments about us and possibly even could draw a picture on a canvas of what she envisions us to be. However, she will most easily be able to describe our thoughts and insights offered in the conversation.

We can go further in escaping our physical by reading stories in the Bible. Regardless of our personal beliefs, we will soon begin to envision the authors in physical terms, but will be more drawn to emphasize their ideas and concepts. While the concepts are still manifestations of the physical, they are closer to the spiritual. To enjoy Sabbath living, we need to examine what, in all the physicality that we have experienced, meshes with the truth in our soul.

In I Peter 4ff, the author emphasizes the need for us to consider that "though [we] are judged in the flesh as men, [we] may live in the spirit according to the will of God." The will of God is infinite happiness and brings to fruition all as He has decreed. In considering these virtues of God, we cannot fail to have the greatest admiration and love for this One who is our only court of resort. As we always live in the spirit, we must live joyously.

Throughout his writings Paul underscores this need for us to be joyous even in our physical distress but in no place is he more uncompromising than in Romans 8:1ff:

> There is now no condemnation for those who live in Christ Jesus, for the law of the Spirit of God has set you free from the law of sin and death....God did: sending His own Son in the likeness of sinful flesh and as an offering for sin, He condemned sin in the flesh...For the mind set on the flesh is death, but the mind set on the Spirit is life and peace...you are not in the flesh but in the Spirit, if indeed the Spirit of God dwells in you.

Here Paul is unmistakable in his assertion that we are spiritual and not physical beings. He has experienced the divine judgment of Christ-God and the redemptive healing that followed. While Paul still bears the sickening knowledge of his brutal murdering of the early saints of Christendom, he also lives in the fullness of God's eternal forgiveness. Our physical manifestation is but an opportunity for us to express our love to God and our fellow spiritual brothers and sisters. Thus, we are to copy after Jesus Himself, and taking Jesus for our precedent, make ourselves like Him, who is all perfection and all happiness. The only possible way that this can happen is through the will of God.

Recently, one of the sweetest and dearest men I have ever met wrote out a testimony which illustrates how beautiful Sabbath living can be even in meager circumstances. While Perry does not identify himself as such, he well could be the one hundredth sheep for whom the shepherd searched until it was found. Maybe he is an angel who is announcing Christ's presence with us.

My name is Perry Murphy and my number is-------and the one before was a C-number which I'm not sure of at this time---Anyway between those two numbers and my youth commission years, I have over 30 years of confinement, which mean, I have been in prison, longer than I have been on the streets.

I've always believed in God, but never put any effort into living a Godly life until one night about 1 or 2 in the morning. I walked out of the Rockwell Projects on Western & Jackson after drinking and drugging for three days without eating. Now, in my mind, I'm on my way to Greek town to make me some money, and Greek town is the closest place where I can come up--So now, I'm walking down Madison from Western, looking all sad and feeling like a fool. Before I got to Dame and Madison, my stomach reminded me that I hadn't eaten in three whole days. Now, I'm really sick and feeling bad----It's cold outside and is trying to rain.

I am so hungry and beat down, until with tears in my eyes from my own sadness and shame, I started talking to God. I had always been doing those foxhole prayers, whenever I've gotten myself in a fix, but this I can't say that it was a foxhole prayer or not. Because, I was seriously hungry and cold as well. As I was walking down Madison, when I got by the Bull's Stadium, something lead me over to one of the garbage cans and said, 'Pick up that bag on top of the other garbage.' I picked the bag up and right away, I never seen a bag like this one ever before. Inside the bag was a full three-piece chicken dinner-macaroni and cheese, cole slaw and two biscuits. Now, in my mind I'm thinking "Lucky," but yet, I looked up and said, "Thank you, God."

Now there is no place to sit down across from the stadium, so I'm thinking how good this would be if I had a pop. While standing at the red light at the next corner, looking across the street where I was thinking about stopping and eating my chicken dinner, I see a pop can sitting on this little wall by the school. As I walked up I seen the pop can was not open, I picked the can up and shook it out of disbelief. Then, I looked around for other people who might say, 'It's theirs.' However there is nobody around, I decided not to eat there.

So, I started walking real fast before somebody did appear and say that the pop was theirs. In about the middle of the block, I stopped at a light pole which had a little brick around it where I could sit down and eat. I've gotten a full three-piece chicken dinner and a cold can of Dr. Pepper to wash my meal down. I eat everything, but one piece of the chicken. I wrapped it up and put it in my pocket. Even though it was cold outside and starting to rain, I don't remember my chicken dinner being cold at all.

Now, as I continued to walk down Madison in my mind, I'm still on my way to Greek town to make me some money. But, for some reason, I ended up all the way downtown in the loop. It's colder downtown in the loop--It's colder down-town and my body is really tired. I remembered an alley that has warm air blowing out from the building and out of the way of the rain. So, now I'm no longer thinking of money, for I need to rest my body.

I looked until I found the alley, but when I walked back there it was somebody else in the spot. Now back here in this dark alley, my mind told me to make some noise to wake the other man up and see what happens because I now must lay down. I make the noise and the other man jumped up asking me what time it was. I lied and said that it was around six in the morning. He jumped out of the warm spot where he had been laying on some cardboard boxes. I jumped right in there taking off one of the coats I was wearing to cover-up with and went right to sleep.

Thunder and lightening woke me up, it's just starting to get day light outside. I got up and walked out of the alley to the streets. There stood another man who looked like I felt last night. I asked him if he was hungry. He said 'Yes.' I reached down in my pocket and gave him the piece of chicken I had wrapped up last night. I pointed down the alley and told him about the warm spot with the cardboard boxes, one of my coats I had left, and a R.C. left by the man before me. The guy said thanks and went down the alley getting out of the rain.

I felt good behind that and when I started thinking---None of my night was lucky. It was God carrying me and leading me, pointing out to me how He has always watched over me with His kindness and mercy. I've been shot up fourteen times on four different occasions and not once did God leave me. Not once did I say thanks from my heart. But today, I always say, 'Thank you, God,' from my heart for I'm learning to recognize God's voice even through the confusion of this world in which we live. I realize that God is nearby leading and guiding me throughout each day.

I'm now working hard to change my attitude so that I can develop the patience which is needed in order for me to truly do all the things that's required of me by God. I truly want from my heart to help others, so that they don't stay blind as long as I was blind. Daily, I seek God's wisdom and knowledge.

Perry is now realizing that God's presence in his life is continuous and powerful. He has lived where few survive. He has lived in the most impoverished conditions and now is becoming aware that all the time, God has lived with him. He desires to praise and thank God for keeping him company. Can we share out of our plenty as Perry has shared?

Do we realize that we are living with God every split second of our eternity? We are supplied with all our needs before we ask them to be met. Why do we fret so when we are faced with a new challenging opportunity? Why do we even worry that we will be walking this new trail alone? New trails and life changes need to be approached with excitement and joy. We may fail a thousand times before we learn how to climb. Failure is not the sin. Sinning is refusing to try.

Robert Frost wrote a great poem about choosing the road less traveled, however unless he was bi-locational, how could he know that the other road was less traveled? If the road were already there, maybe only the entrance to it indicated what he assumed to be the truth. Do we often also assume that we are carrying a heavier burden than others? This assumption and others are our chains that keep us from enjoying the view during our eternal walk in the Sabbath with God.

Many of us have learned Maslow's Hierarchy of Needs theory either in our private reading or in a sociology or psychology class and have adopted beliefs based upon the various stages. We may have looked with pride at the level to which we have ascended. Another extremely intelligent scholar, Robert Merkle, adapted Maslow's ideas into an Expanded Our Worlds concept, which he subtitled Merkle's Circles. Merkle also subscribed to the concept that as we rise through these Worlds, we gain greater insight into our lives and their meaning (see Chart 4:1).

EXPANDING OUR WORLDS

SEEING/PAROUSIA
(EMERGING)

SEEKING/PLANETARY SUCCESS
(CONVERGING)

Redesign   Microscopic   Outer   Aesthetic   Higher Mental Capacity

STUDYING/PERSONAL SUCCESS
(SUCCEEDING)

Job   Marriage   Ego   Money   Body   Community   Beliefs

SOCIALIZING/PERSONAL RELATIONSHIPS
(BELONGING)

Companionship   Cooperation   Competition   Conflict   Coercion

SENSATIONS/PLEASURES
ENTERTAINING

Pleasure   Pressure   Pain

SURVIVAL/PROVISIONS
(BELONGING)

Work   Rest (welfare)

My experience has taught me a much different lesson. Years ago, as I sat with Grandmother Button on her front porch after a rain, she told me to go into the street and pick up a stone and toss it into a puddle. I did so, and then she said, "Look at the rings coming from where the stone entered the water. You can see that they move out from the middle; this is to show us that God is the center of all of life and His goodness radiates throughout all creation. As you grow and eventually get married, you will realize that on the first ring from the center will be your wife and you, on the second will be your children, and on the third the rest of your family. The remaining rings symbolize all the rest of your God-given brothers and sisters in the world. Your responsibility is to love God first, your bride second, and so on."

As I have contemplated the truth of the words of each of these wonderful people, I have realized that we can and often will sacrifice our lower needs and desires for higher physical, mental, and spiritual goals. We can be selfish or self-giving, believing or despairing, emerging or submerging. We can destroy the opportunities God gives us as a child destroys a toy. We cannot create, but we can discover the creations God places before us.

In our discovery of these creations, we will choose to throw off many of the personal comforts and physically pleasing gifts for dangerous and physically demanding lifestyles. This can happen in a moment when we see another human in extreme danger. We may rush into a burning building or dive into icy waters. We may die physically at that instant with the one we are trying to save, but we will live as spiritual examples of persons whose lives mattered.

There are at least two factors that determine the quality and quantity of our commitment and participation in God's will for our lives. The first and most important factor is our maturity in understanding Divine love. In I Peter 4:1-2, 6, and 2:1-2 we are told:

> Therefore, since Christ has suffered in the flesh, arm yourselves also with the same purpose, because he who has suffered in the flesh has ceased from sin, so to live the rest of the time in the flesh no longer for the lusts of men, but for the will of God...For the gospel has for this purpose been preached even to those who are dead, that though they are judged in the flesh as men [and women], they may live in the spirit according to the will of God.
>
> Therefore, putting aside all malice and all guile and hypocrisy

and envy and all slander, like newborn babies, long for the pure milk of the word, that by it you may grow in respect to salvation…

I have often read and heard that we mature from self-preservation to the more mature understanding of agape love. I suggest that we need instead to believe and practice the truth that pure love has been in our souls from creation. Our requirement is to draw on the wellspring of that love. I also caution you from believing that there are three kinds of love: agape, philia, and eros. The latter two are usually considered as brotherly love and self-aggrandizing behavior and definitely not God-love. I suggest that all love is of God.

When we live expressing love, we are strongly motivated to grow in the knowledge of how best to accomplish this desire. We also reflect this in our attitude adjustments. These attitude changes usually are exhibited with movement from an almost exclusive to a more universal viewpoint. When our knowledge increases and our attitude reflects growth toward a more loving spiritual and physical manner, we then participate with greater proficiency in God's plan for our lives.

Secondly, God has fashioned us with the eternal knowledge of His perfection. He has allowed us to envision the perfect and has placed us in the physical bodies we occupy to test our willingness to stand on that peak of His perfection. We always will be restless until we have accepted and are willing to use the climbing suit we have been given. Only when we dedicate ourselves to the adventure, do we realize that we are provided with everything we need to achieve our dream.

While we are climbing, we will seek out survival skills and provisions to supply us on our journey, but will find that God has supplied all our needs. We will then experience pain, pleasure, and pressure in our quest. We will decide if we can go it alone or if we need help and how we will treat those whom we enlist in our eternal climb. We may take steps that will cause us to slide back down the trail or throw disappointment into another's journey, but we will desire to get back up and begin again.

Expanding our awareness of the eternal world in which we have been placed by God is both frightening and exhilarating. It is frightening because we are in unknown territory. We will worry over the next step, for it may be our last. We may tumble to the bottom of the crevasse, we may be stretched to the mental breaking point, or we may discover that the gods we worshiped cannot satisfy our needs. How terrible if we live most of our physical lives only to discover we have been worshiping idols. We might then ask ourselves if we wasted all this time and have nothing but rag dolls to show for it. Will we go on with our fantasy even knowing we have been worshiping pipe dreams?

I have observed men who are incarcerated and who have been in prison on several previous convictions. I have frequently detected in their behavior and speech a mournful resignation to their perceived condition and a reluctance to accept that they are participants and not victims in life. They can still be forced to talk victorious living, however their eyes and body movements tell a story of defeat. I sometimes compare their attitudes and behavior to old men in wheelchairs sitting in nursing homes waiting for physical death. I have also seen these same inmates accept that their sins have been forgiven and become like newborn babies desiring the milk of life. This is very wonderful!

While I believe that forty percent to fifty percent of those who are sentenced to incarceration pose enough of a threat to society that a period of time behind bars or fences is necessary, the remainder who occupy our prisons do so because both they and we are failing to live out our God-given purpose. When we fail to believe that every person is a child of God, and thus treat them as misfits and excess baggage, we destroy opportunities to honor and love God. We need to live in the Sabbath, praising God and honoring each of our fellow brothers and sisters. Too often, we have viewed death and killing from biblical times to the present as approved by God.

We have become so calloused to killing, such as the abortion of babies, that we have incarcerated ourselves in the mistakes of our ancestors. Are we doomed to live their failure by accepting killing, death, and punishment as necessary to life? Can we begin again to view conception as a God blessing, which involves the man's sperm, the woman's egg, and God placing the spirit in the womb? Will a day arrive when capital punishment will be seen as a continuation of violence, rather than as a solution to previous killing?

We should realize that killing always results in more killing. Individual killing almost always leads to group killing. This escalates to massive wars, which require nations to overpower aggressors in order to affect peace. However, peace never comes from war. War can be won, peace cannot.

As humans, we may always believe that we need to war on one another until we can accept that we all are brothers and sisters by creation and redemption. If this appears to be depressing, we need to ask ourselves, "How may we break the bounds of our despair? How can we learn that we live in the richness of God's mercy and forgiveness? What must we do to inherit the kingdom of God?"

In I Peter 2:1ff, we are instructed to put aside everything that confuses us and long for the "pure milk of the word" that we "may grow in respect to [our] salvation." For we "are a chosen race, a royal priesthood, a holy nation, a people for God's own possession." To whom is Peter referring? Does he mean only a few gathered at the church of our ancestors, or does he mean all of the race of humans for whom Christ-God died?

As we ponder these questions for answers that possibly will quell our anxious spirits, let us find a quiet place that is away from the noise of life. Let us sit and seek to discover the most immense and unexplored world that touches us all, the world of silence. In this complex world we do so many things by speech and action that we can become insensitive to the power and influence of silence. We often connect uselessness with silence and think noise and action mean fruitfulness and service. In this day of insecurity and suffering, what we urgently need is to realize that there is something vital in stillness. It restores, rebuilds, and renews the very fabric of our soul.

Consider the vast, strange world inside each of us, the world of thought, reason, memory; of faith and fear, hope and despair; of the heart's marvelous action and the chemistry of the body hushed and still. Listen to yourself breathe. Feel the blood rushing through your veins. Hear in the silence the movement of the wind. One of our greatest gifts from God is silence. If we desire greater nearness to God, we need to become more silent. Silence is never stagnant nor idle. Silence enables God to take possession of our lives, to give us His life, His peace, His strength, and His wisdom.

Now we are prepared to continue our pilgrimage. We will sometimes harm ourselves and others. We will quit a thousand times only to begin again. We will discard the trivial, the important, the necessary, and the unnecessary only to find that God is always placing the survival gear we need in our hands. This eternal journey in living is the essence of life itself. It is our freedom and liberty to discover our value as children of God. Do we cherish our freedom? Are we honoring God's faith in us?

In the previous chapters, I have been able to identify landmarks that explained the concepts that defined that particular area of Christocentric truth. However, the concept of living with freedom and liberty in the Sabbath of God is as extensive as the seven billion people on Earth and the unknown trillions living on other Earths in the universe. Over many years, I have learned that the stories of Jesus express this truth the best.

One of the parables Jesus told illustrates our position in God's kingdom. In Matthew 21:33ff, Jesus relates a story about a landowner who turns land over to farmers who agreed to raise crops on it and return a portion of the crop to the owner. Recently, Dr. William A. Ritter, pastor of the First United Methodist Church in Birmingham, Michigan, related a modernized version of the story:

> A landowner purchased several thousand acres of land in the state of Michigan. However, he was a cattleman who lived in Texas and had thousands of head of cattle to care for. He needed experts who had the knowledge, experience, and capability to care for the apple and peach orchards that grew on this Michigan land.
>
> Hence, he advertised, interviewed, and contracted with some persons whom he believed would best care for his new purchase and the crop that would be produced. The agreement, which both signed, required that at harvest the owner would send semi-trailer trucks to collect his portion of the apples and peaches. The rest of the crop could then be sold by the sharecroppers for their profit.
>
> This agreement worked pretty well for the first three years; however, on the fourth season when the trucks arrived, the sharecroppers pulled the drivers out of the trucks, beat them, burned their trucks, and left them on the highway to die. The state police came along and took the injured men to the hospital where two recovered and the other three died. Upon investigating the problem, the authorities discovered that certain irregularities surrounded the case and decided to prosecute the case no further.
>
> The fifth year, the owner sent more truckers and semis to collect his portion of the crop. These were treated even more brutally. The subsequent investigation revealed that the truckers had come to Michigan looking to start a ruckus in order to settle the previous years hostility.
>
> The sixth year, the landowner sent his son along to ensure that the crop was correctly collected. This time the sharecroppers wanted to send a message down to Texas, so they killed the son, threw him in the back of one of the trucks and sent him and

all of the rotten apples and peaches they could get in the trucks back to Texas. When the trucks returned, the landowner ran out and opened the first van. Out fell the fruit, the stench, and eventually out came the body of the son. All the neighbors counseled the father to send the Texas Rangers up to Michigan and to do to them what they had done to his son.

The father, replied to all his friends, "Don't you know what the truth is in these matters? My son is a monument to the truth and those who believe that they can confiscate the landowners property shall know who truly owns the land. My son will forever deliver this message to all who would occupy my land."

We need to know that Christ indeed does deliver the message to us that God owns all existence. We have been given the vision by God to see the Parousia (knowing one is redeemed and standing in the presence of the God-Christ). We have been given the vision to know His presence is existence. As we exist in God's Sabbath, we are to occupy God's land, to buy and sell it, and to assume ownership by holding title to it, yet as we do so we always must know that everything is owned by God. If we conceive that we are separated from God and able to do as we desire with no judgment, we are building castles in the air. The very knowledge of God dictates that we are not able to wander in God's kingdom as innocents, but are responsible for our decisions. Living Christocentrically is a wonderful privilege. It's truth will excite us as we awaken each morning. As we face each opportunity, it will appear as if we have been born anew every day! Then, we will discover the meaning that Eleanor Fiock found:

> Whoever walks a mountain trail has never walked alone,
> Or lifted eyes unto the hills but inner strength has known,
> Whoever seeks communion sweet in God's Cathedral there,
> Will find the angels very near and joining him in prayer.
> Whoever walks a mountain trail or kneels upon the sod,
> Has been so near to heaven's gate, he touched the hand of God.

We can physically walk the mountains and commune with God, however we need to walk those mountains spiritually before we can discover the virtue of the physical journey. We can discover if, when, and how often we live in the spiritual and translate this living to the physical by examining ourselves neurolinguistically. This is accomplished by our understanding the concept and then applying it to our reasoning and to our behavior patterns.

Neurolinguistics has five distinct features: first, it is defined by the perfect circle. The circle is the eternity of God in which we have been created and within which we live. The other four features occupy distinct and exclusive areas of the circle. Emotions or feelings are located on the lower-right quadrant. Ideals, values, and ethereal truths are positioned on the upper-right quadrant. Analytical or critical factors are positioned in the upper-left quadrant. Organizational and structural ingredients are in the lower-left quadrant (see Chart 4:2).

NEUROLINGUISTICS
WHOLE-BRAINED ACTIVITY
The circle is the eternity of God

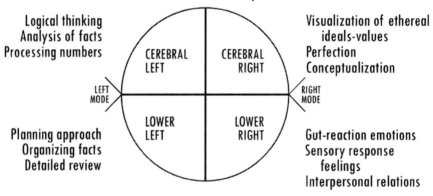

Logical thinking
Analysis of facts
Processing numbers

CEREBRAL LEFT

CEREBRAL RIGHT

LEFT MODE

RIGHT MODE

LOWER LEFT

LOWER RIGHT

Visualization of ethereal ideals-values
Perfection
Conceptualization

Planning approach
Organizing facts
Detailed review

Gut-reaction emotions
Sensory response
feelings
Interpersonal relations

As children of God, we have the entire neurolinguistics structure in our spiritual bodies. However, as in other gifts given to us by God, we often have not made use of them in our physical bodies. Most persons that I have observed in prison use only the two elements on the right side of the circle, that is, the emotions and the ideal. While it is good that they have at least discovered these two gifts, the fact that they are only aware of these results in their lives being lived as though they were a ping pong ball bouncing back and forth between the two quadrants.

I have found that these persons always let their physical control their spiritual. They bounce between feelings and ideals. Their physical features will be expressive of anger, hate, love, joy, happiness as they move toward the ideal.

Then, they will compare these feelings with the way they envision the perfect. The bounce-back to emotions will eventually result in frustration, disappointment, and despair. Their eyes and head will also move up and down to the right as if they are prohibited from any other movement.

We can quickly discover this by listening to the language patterns, by watching the head and eye movements, and by observing the rage and despair exhibited by one so fixated. Their language will often degenerate into disgustingly vile swearing. More moderate language will contain statements that begin with, "I feel" or "Things shouldn't be that way."

I have found that a person caught in this trap can be helped by first conversing, using language appropriate to his quadrant area. If he uses feeling language, I would ask him to explain the feeling in more depth, as in, "What causes you to be so angry?" Regardless of his answer, I begin to assist him in his trip around the circle by asking, "How do you believe this could be solved most ideally?"

After he answers, I then ask him to analyze how these two thoughts could be resolved? (I usually do not use the word analyze because he may feel threatened. However, I will use it for the sake of this brief description. It will help to demonstrate how understanding neurolinguistic activity and focusing on the upper left quadrant expands our understanding of Christocentric truth.) Following his answer, I work with him to organize steps to reach a resolution of this problem.

It is essential to work at a speed that doesn't cause the person to become confused or fearful. As the person participates in the process, he will begin to cock his head in the proper direction and his eyes will follow along. Once the individual becomes accustomed to this 360 degree neurolinguistic experience, he will discover greater peace in his life and will seek to use this soul gift consistently. Unless this neurolinguistic mode is used, both individuals and groups will continue to live imprisoned in the physical while wondering why happiness is so impossible or transitory. We need to believe that, as perfect children of God, we are called to submit ourselves to "pick up our cross and follow Christ." I believe that our cross is most often the physical body, which includes nerves, muscles, and organs, which need to be in submission to our spirit.

The difference between God and us is that God is infinitely happy and we are not. God's infinite love flows from all His truth and actions. However, we often live as though God has abandoned us to an evil existence. In I John 4:19 we read, "We love because He first loved us." Consequently, our ability to serve and love God and our brothers and sisters will be in proportion to our understanding and realization of His goodness and love. God expects all of us to know our responsibilities in this world.

In Genesis 2:17, Adam and Eve were advised of the consequences of eating the fruit from the center of the Garden. Whatever the fruit is, it was meant by God to be irresistible and impossible to be refused or ignored. In John 10:1-18, Jesus Christ further clarifies His position in our lives. We are able to participate in Sabbath living only as He prescribes. If we attempt to manufacture our own life choices, we are considered as robbers, thieves, and murderers. Christ has eternal life for us to live. We can have it in abundance if we, as God's sheep, follow the program as it is and not as we would imagine it to be. Do we believe that we live in the Sabbath of God? Is God's eternity complete and eternal? Are we part of that eternity? Has God ever needed to remodel any of His eternity? Is what happens after we leave the physical body, commonly called heaven, all there is to eternity?

How you and I answer these questions determines our present happiness and peace and our willingness to view the choices offered to us as either holy or damning. Are we desiring to eat from God's hand the fruit of our eternal lives and live?

We will experience the never-ending challenges of this new world. They will be challenges that can inspire us to search for peace, happiness, meaningful relationships, and especially acceptance from God and others, while we are surrounded by "tribulation, or distress, or persecution, or famine, or nakedness, or peril, or sword" (Romans 8:35).

Choosing to leave the sterile environs of our yesterdays and entering the dynamic of today includes accepting that "For Thy sake we are killed all the day long; we are accounted as sheep for the slaughter, [yet] in all these things, we are more than conquerors through him that loved us, [consequently nothing] shall be able to separate us from the love of God in Christ Jesus our Lord" (selected from Romans 8:36-39). Christ is the shepherd who takes us to new and unknown pastures in order that we may experience new tests in the rewarding experience of living.

Christ, in God, goes before us. In Psalm 17, we, with David, confess that we have walked on the wild side, refusing God's intended path for us, yet we desire that God make things right again. We desire salvation from our lies and wandering ways. Nevertheless, we continue to envy those who have material blessings. We are unwilling to enjoy our perfect relationship with God. Instead, we are captivated by external attractions. In Isaiah 53:1ff, we have this wonderful truth from God. God is asking us, "Who has believed our message?" We should answer, "I believe! I believe that you, God, are greater in stature than any god I could conceive. I believe that I am safe on this trip on Spaceship Earth, and I will man my station as you guide us through the eternal universe."

In concluding this chapter, Don Knight, a fellow student in seminary, wrote and gave me this unpublished poem:

THE MAN
I stood on top of the world;
The whole earth beneath me,
The sky above me,
Clouds all around me.
I stood and gazed at the kingdoms of men,
Turning slowly to see the world
And then I saw the man.

It was a strange feeling
He did nothing—just stood looking at me smiling gently.
He looked so...He stretched out his hand,
and I turned and ran
ran as fast as my legs would carry me,
down the mountain,
out of the clouds,
back among
the kingdoms of men.

I have traveled many miles since then. I have seen great
cathedrals made of costly stone, with jeweled crosses and
"wealth" written a cross their altars.

I have walked along country lanes where birds always seemed
to sing, and the wayside flowers laughed in the morning as they
tossed their heads to the passing breeze.

I have eased my tired feet in mountain streams,
slept covered with the scent of hay,
loved in the warm secrets of a woman's heart
but I never saw the man again...until...

I saw a child, huddled against a stone wall in a
large city where people passed—but never smiled,
and talked—but never spoke
and moved—but never lived—
a child whose eyes seemed full of all the pain the world had
ever known, crouching cold and frightened
in a corner for the warmth of the stones...
and I bent to speak and could
not say what was in my heart—but my eyes spoke for me with
their tears...

And as I turned to go my way
burdened with the body of the child,
I saw the man, standing with His arms opened wide...
and I ran to Him,
and He to me,

And we have walked together since that day—
The Man
the child
and me!

God bless you every today of your eternal life!

CHAPTER 5
Flourishing in Our Choosing

I did not start out writing this book with the intention of instructing you on how you could improve your life. I cannot imagine that you would be receptive to a change in the format at this juncture, so I will proceed with explaining how I discovered who I am. This process began very early in my life, most likely before I even was aware of it.

I was blessed to have parents who were very goal-directed people. I remember that I often did not appreciate this fact. They believed that their children should excel in life, and as many other parents who survived the Depression, they wanted a better life for their children. I was the second child born to Marion and Nelda Button, and the first son. My sister, Lois, and I had four years to be the focus of attention before the next child, Nancy, would enter the picture. Hence, Lois and I received the initial parental training, which was intended to guide us into our youth as obedient and well-disciplined children. Our parents' discipline probably would be judged as too repressive today; however, in the years surrounding the Second World War, their concern came within the context of that evil era.

Just like Isaac, I was circumcised by my eighth day, and my sister and I were baptized as infants. Our religious education was also begun at birth. We were enrolled in Sunday school from the time we were infants, and to my knowledge we never missed a summer Bible school all through junior high school. I can honestly confess that I did not enjoy having my summers shortened by the Bible school interruption.

My father was a very intelligent man who had won a full four-year scholarship to any state college in Illinois when he was only in the eighth grade. However, due to the Depression, he was able to go to only one semester of college before he had to return home and help his parents. In 1936 he and my mother married. A year later he became a father. His struggle with not being able to fulfill his academic aspirations because of limited resources and parental responsibilities had to be a life-long frustration. These factors undoubtedly played into my parents' determination to have Phillip and Lois go to college.

Both my sister and I believed that we were held to a higher standard of behavior than other children seemed to be. We would ask for permission to go to a movie or a program that other kids our same age were attending and frequently were given the parental one-word answer, "No!" When we protested and said, "All the other kids in the neighborhood are going," we would be told, "You are not all the other kids in the neighborhood!" This didn't mean that our parents were wrong in their decision; it just meant that they were our parents.

Both my parents taught me the meaning of espousal dedication. Their example of love and devotion as a daily part of living has been a great gift to me in my marriage to my wife, Jane. This was exemplified by praising one another, regularly kissing each other, and forever refusing even to harbor a negative thought, either spoken or otherwise displayed physically. I am forever thankful to them and have enjoyed the benefits throughout the over forty-four years of marriage to the bride that God gave me to love and esteem.

I have already told you about my vision when I was nine. The announcement of it only added fuel to the fire of parental focus. While I was by no means the perfect child in my behavior, I perceived that I was always taking a few too many wacks on the posterior. This resulted in my perception of my father as rigid and harsh, which interfered with a close father-son relationship. He wanted a son who was compliant and well-disciplined, and I wanted not to be afraid of him. This eventually resulted in deceptive rebellion on my part, which further aggravated our relationship. It also hindered my progress in other areas, such as school grades, sports competition, and peer relationships.

In fairness to both my father and mother, I was allowed a great deal of freedom to grow up as normally as a child could while World War II was going on. I had a paper route from age nine, was given considerable freedom in the spending of my money, and was allowed to roam the neighborhood growing up like most of the other boys.

Following my sophomore year in high school, I was chosen to go to a Methodist youth congress at Purdue University in Indiana. This was the first time that I had visited a college campus and the first time that I had been with five thousand other young people.

Along with this great experience came my first introduction to a bookstore. I didn't realize that one could buy books and take them home. Previously I had only checked books out of the public library. Among those that I bought was a book written by British writer, J. B. Phillips. While I have long since forgotten the contents of the book, I vividly remember its title, *Your God Is Too Small*.

This title has been a constant encouragement to me, both in my ministry and in my personal life, because I had grown up with a very provincial religious faith. I envisioned God as a stern judge and Jesus as a friend who would rescue me from my problems. When I discovered that this belief was childish, I was determined to read and study the Word to search out a more valid God to worship.

As I began to make better choices, my focus on the place that God occupied in my life expanded. I began to have a clearer image of what a relationship with God meant. I also began to mature in my relationship with my father. This happened in a very unexpected place and in a way I never would have imagined.

At the end of my second year in college, I decided to return to my home in Kewanee, Illinois, and to work for a while in the same factory where my father had spent the major portion of his life working. Since I knew my time there would be only six to nine months, I went to work and enjoyed every minute. I even tried to set new records at various assembly assignments.

One day, I reported for work and was assigned to be the helper to my father on a very large shear machine. I admit that I was a bit apprehensive when I was told that we were to work together. Following my father's directions, I was to help in such a way that the steel we cut into pieces was done correctly and with due speed. If I failed to do as instructed, a great deal of money could have been lost in producing scrap steel and possibly one of us could have been hurt or killed.

I remember that it was a hot summer day and that there was a full day's work to be done. I was sweating even before we started, but I was determined to do well. Two things happened that day. First, I heard my father curse for the first time in my life. It was not the moderate word that he used that commanded my attention, but that he used any curse word at all. I nearly died! I thought to myself, "My father is human!"

The second important thing happened at the end of the day. As we were riding home together, my father said, "I really enjoyed having you as my helper today. I have had hundreds of helpers and I would class you as the best that I have ever had working with me." He then went on to explain exactly why I had been so good to work with on that project. I thanked him for telling me what he felt about my ability to work with him, but deep inside I was jumping up and down with joy.

As I reflect on this early growing-up period of my life, I discover that I was blessed with having parents who were so dedicated to having their children be exemplary that they supervised and judged their children's behavior with vigor. I also am confident that they believed that ample amounts of forgiveness and love were being passed out. I do know, however, that every time we came from visiting our grandparents, my mother and father expressed great concern that we had been "spoiled" and needed a bit of reality therapy to get us on the right path again.

From my point of view, I wanted a friend in my father, one whom I respected yet who would be willing to have me crawl up on his lap, to wrap his arms around me, and to tell me a story. I did not see this side of him until Jane and I had children. They crawled all over my father, and he loved it. Of course, these were his grandchildren. It was permissible and even a requirement to be loving and lenient. In 1976, my father died suddenly of a massive heart attack while my mother and he were on their fortieth wedding anniversary trip to Hawaii. While we had gotten to be friends, I still would have chosen for us to have become real pals. I love having my mother still around at eighty-seven for me to hug and kiss every time we are together.

That series of months with me living at home and working with my father in the factory ended with my marriage to Jane in December 1958. This event began major steps in my moving forward into the ministry and our moving into parenthood. The lessons of living life from the parent side of the equation began in October 1959 with the birth of our first daughter, Patricia. It continued in May 1961 and eleven months later in April 1962 with the arrival of our two sons, James and Michael. Then in September 1965 we welcomed Cathleen as our fourth and last child.

I also realized that my God was growing in size as I began to pastor two churches. I do not know what those wonderful people learned about God, but since I was forced to prepare to preach each Sunday, I learned to read the Bible for something meaningful to say. I believed that I was very good at preaching sermons and teaching biblical truths. I also received a fair amount of praise, which confirmed my own evaluation. The best praise is from someone who tells how a sermon helped them in a life issue a year or more after the sermon was preached.

I moved on from those two small churches, learning both to preach and to pastor a little better in each pastorate over the next thirty years. The pastoring often becomes more important than the preaching. Often, pastoring involves helping churches and committees make difficult decisions. These committees are filled with people attempting to guide the congregation in safe paths. They sometimes are required to make difficult decisions. This can lead to conflict with the pastor, who may believe a radical change of course is necessary.

This is exactly what happened at the church I was serving prior to accepting the chaplaincy at the correctional center. I believe that leadership can and often will require the pastor to take paths that may not be joyously received at the time and that may direct the one suggesting those changes to depart for another pasture. Maybe this is God's way of shepherding us through eternity.

As a result, in 1984 I arrived at the Jacksonville Correctional Center to begin a new ministry, one that God had been preparing me to do for all the previous years of my life. I am certain of this because I do not remember ever having harboured a desire to become a prison chaplain prior to the months leading up to that moment of acceptance.

One day, as I was teaching a Bible class in the prison, we turned to the book of Matthew for our study. My intent was to teach a lesson; however, I soon discovered that I was to be taught by God that I now needed to further expand my vision of Him. The Scripture was Matthew 19:16-24. It began as Jesus was approached by a man who desired positive confirmation that the way that he had been living his life was correct.

> And behold, one came to Him and said, "Teacher, what good thing shall I do that I may obtain eternal life?"
>
> And He said to him, "Why are you asking Me about what is good? There is only One who is good; but if you wish to enter into life keep the commandments."
>
> He said to Him, "Which ones?"
>
> And Jesus said, "You shall not commit murder; you shall not commit adultery; you shall not steal; you shall not bear false witness; honor your father and mother; and you shall love your neighbor as yourself."
>
> The young man said to Him, "All these things I have kept; what am I still lacking?"
>
> Jesus said to him, "If you wish to be complete, go and sell

your possessions and give to the poor, and you shall have treasure in heaven; and come, follow Me." But when the young man heard this statement, he went away grieved; for he was one who owned much property.

And Jesus said to His disciples, "Truly I say to you, it is hard for a rich man to enter the kingdom of heaven. And again I say to you, it is easier for a camel to go through the eye of a needle than for a rich man to enter the kingdom of God."

I had read and taught this story many times; however, on this day I was that man who was asking Jesus the question. I became determined not to go away grieved. I wanted to experience the completeness that Jesus was talking about. I knew that He was not talking to me about money or keeping the commandments. Jesus was talking about the illusions that I needed to throw aside in order to live a spiritual life experience with the Christ.

In order for me to begin living and understanding the Bible spiritually, I needed to begin to live the biblical truths. I looked to I Corinthians, Chapter 5. In these thirteen verses, Paul was writing to one of the churches he had founded about a man who had taken his father's wife for himself. The message had appeared to me to be very straightforward and easy to understand when I previously had read it as a physical problem.

However, when I read it again spiritually, it had quite a different message. The message related to the lesson that Jesus taught the rich ruler. Jesus said to him, and to me, that we cannot mix spiritual truths with physical ones. The spiritual truth is that as children of God, we are perfect. We are eternally saved and cannot do anything to change this truth. The physical truth is that we always feel judged and in jeopardy of missing out on the great blessings in life.

I learned that I am a spiritual being created and perfected by God and placed in a physical suit. My responsibility as a spiritual being is to direct me physically as God has commanded me. I can best illustrate this challenge by using a physical issue with which I deal daily.

The men to whom I minister in Jacksonville Prison are there for crimes they have been convicted of committing. I could approach them from the perspective of convicts, and I would be correct because they have been convicted. I could judge them for being rapists, child molesters, murderers, drug manufacturers, or any of a hundred felonious crimes, and I would be correct because I have access to their files. If I do this I am participating in a physical ministry. If I mix this information with the spiritual and identify them as God's sinful children, then I will be mixing leaven in the lump of dough.

The mixing of leaven in the lump of dough is explained in Matthew 16:6, when Jesus Christ warned against mixing physical activities with spiritual truths and believing they are equivalent. In Galatians 5:9 and I Corinthians 5:6, Paul discredits any belief that emphasizes physical acts, such as circumcision, as being necessary to effect the salvation of Christ.

The spiritual truth is that the inmates are perfect children of God, eternally forgiven by God in Christ, and set free to choose how to live their perfection. The difficulty in teaching this truth is that all the other fine children of God are telling them that they are lost to hell if they do not accept Christ as their Savior, get baptized, and dedicate themselves to serving the Lord all the remaining days of their lives. Since this is the universal mantra only slightly dressed in different clothing depending on the particular denomination, the voice of one chaplain in a prison often does not carry much weight.

Fortunately, the truth is the truth, and the truth will win out. The lie can never win for more than a little while and then deceives itself in the telling. You will understand this if you believe that God is perfect and can create no imperfection. Hence, we are perfect souls living in clay bodies with the purpose of using those clay bodies to express our love to God and our fellow brothers and sisters.

Jesus was talking to me about eternal spiritual living that He knew began with our creation in the sixth day because He was there as God. Jesus told the young man that his emphasis on the legality of keeping the commandments had corrupted his truth. Jesus asked the man to destroy his pride in being successful in observing legalism and to live the truth of the commandments.

I, too, have had to cast off my illusions of putting stars in my crown. I believed I was earning them by sacrificing for the people in various congregations, by suffering in silence the insensitivities of the church hierarchy, and by acting out being a good person. All of these were death knells to my growth as a spiritual person living in a physical world. I am blessed to have a bride who loved me in spite of my martyrdom. She also has rejoiced as I have become more cognizant of Christocentric truth.

What was the rich young ruler's problem? Was mine similar to his? I think so. The simple truth is that we both believed that going about doing good and doing our duty was what life was all about. Neither is life at all. Life is accepting the freedom that God's salvation provides. The freedom to live unafraid of the consequences of failure. Freedom to explore the universe. Freedom to imagine that one can do anything and then to do it. Freedom to believe in oneself, in each other, and in the entirety of God's children in the universe.

Could I throw off my fears and choose to live? I needed only to observe the wonderful lady who in her freedom had loved me for so many great years. A lady who is mother to our four wonderful children and a friend to each of them. A woman who has lived this truth without even worrying if it had a name. I understood when I paused to observe Jane's graceful living with all whom she met.

This has been true throughout the eighteen years that Jane has taught men in the prison. She is a most gifted person and reminds me of the persons Jesus talked about in John 5:24 and following. Here He defines the eternal truth that we have in our midst. We need only live the eternity we are a part of and not deceive ourselves or others that eternity is something one is given later after being good today.

Jane has a classroom of men who have failed at learning thousands of times. She gently and firmly leads them toward a deep honoring of themselves by articulating with her presence a "can do" attitude. Men who have come into her room unable to add or subtract or read even the most basic signs leave after a few months equipped to honor themselves and their families.

Christocentric truth continues as we occupy these physical shells and proceeds until God announces the Omega. In this chapter of John, Jesus was talking about today, which is the one and only day of the Lord. Jesus was talking about the freedom that has been true since before we were created and was effectively illustrated in the Christ who lived, died, and was resurrected for our benefit two thousand years ago. This has become, for me, a message of Christocentric truth, and living in this day of our Lord is Sabbath living.

This chapter is written to assist you in understanding how I have grown in my picture of God and how this has been such a blessing in expanding my horizons to include the universe. It is also my attempt to explain the joy I have realized as we live this Sabbath life. Explaining the freedom God has given us to choose to live spiritually or to allow the physical to dominate life is a wonderful privilege. My reality of God has changed in that I describe the presence of God as eternally judging our every activity, finding us either guilty or innocent, and then redeeming us through the Christ presence. I am less angry that the judgment of God is so active because I now understand the need for me to be constantly confronted with the truth.

Do I conceive of God as a whole-universe God? Much of the religious grounding that I have experienced has been presented with our Earth as the sole habitat of humans and these humans as the sole concern of God. Could I now expand my faith to include a God who has children throughout the entire universe? Might I possibly be only at the beginning of the journey that God has created for all of us and for our yet unknown brothers and sisters? Do I dare believe that if our conflicts, hatreds, and wars were resolved with our fellow family members here on Earth, greater challenges and opportunities would await all of us in our own galaxy and the galaxies beyond?

To all these questions, I would answer a resounding, "Yes!" I am firmly convinced that we are presently parochially viewing the world through blinders, and we need to consider the greater good of all the billions of our fellow astronauts. We need to cease calling persons pagans just because they do not have the same faith orientation as we, and we need to begin to include them in our total plan of exploring the universe. I believe that we have done enough damage to our fellow Earth-dwellers and conversely they have equally injured us enough. I cannot conceive how we can profit each other by continued hatred and killing.

Do I now worship a God of all truth? Can I conceive of a God that is so present with us that if He were to cease thinking about us for a millisecond, we would completely evaporate from existence? Is it feasible to believe that we have always been perfected by and in God? Do I trust God for the total perfection of everyone? Do I believe that our only responsibilities are to love God, to love our fellow brothers and sisters, and even to love ourselves? I am trying to understand the implications of the omnipresent God of us all. I desire to love God and daily practice doing so. I find it far more difficult to love many of my fellow brothers and sisters up close and personal.

When I think about this "love my fellow human" business, I sometimes wonder if maybe it would be easier just to keep the commandments. No killing or robbing or even that adultery business likely would be easier than loving all these people all the time. Can't I take time out once in a while to hate a little? There are some people that I have some issues with, and loving doesn't seem to get it done. Doesn't God have something else that I could do to be complete?

Maybe we could have a special day of the year to love one another. How about Christmas? We can easily love on Christmas, but love everyone every day? Isn't God asking a bit much? I can understand how that young ruler would go away sorrowfully. I know of at least ten people that I have a hard time even liking, let alone loving.

Recently, I received a prayer that was written anonymously representing a possible message given to us by God. Maybe it will provide you with some insight into God's concern for all of us.

> Good Morning.
> I am God. Today I will be handling all of your problems. Please remember that I DO NOT need your help! If the devil happens to deliver a situation to you that you cannot handle, DO NOT attempt to resolve it. Kindly put it in the SFJTD (something for JESUS to do) box. It will be addressed in MY time, not yours. Once the matter is placed into the box, do not hold on to it or attempt to remove it. Holding on or removal will delay the resolution of your problem. If it is a situation that you think you are capable of handling, please consult ME IN PRAYER to be sure that it is the proper resolution. BECAUSE I do not sleep nor do I slumber, there is no need for you to lose any sleep. Rest my child. If you need to contact me, I am only a prayer away.

Everyday I pray that I am willing to "cast my bread on the surface of the waters" so that I will grow in understanding, believing that God is perfect and everything created is perfect. If I learn to live rejoicing in the Lord, convinced that God has already taken care of all that is required to effect our continuous relationship with Him, then I will no longer need to be anxious for what the day might bring. I can enjoy the freedom of total companionship with God and with my fellow citizens of God's kingdom. This is living Christocentric truth in the Sabbath of God.

I believe that loving God is so very critical for our spiritual journey that daily we need to affirm the blessing of God's eternal activity in our lives. I suggest that this can best be done by choosing a biblical verse we can use to guide our minute-by-minute thinking. I am including a few of the thousands of such phrases in the Old Testament and the New Testament, which I use each day. I hope you will be inspired to add more to the list.

I begin each of the phrases with: God, thank you for your blessings today, I affirm Your truth:

Genesis 1:28 God, You bless us.

Genesis 1:28 God, You guide us to be fruitful and multiply.

Genesis 2:18 God, You have made helpers for us.

Genesis 3:4 God, You have given us the choice to be born anew.

Genesis 4:1 God, You have given us Your children to love.

Genesis 22:17 God, You bless us and multiply our seed as the stars.

Leviticus 22:43 Lord, You are our God.

Numbers 10:10 Lord, You have blessed all the works of our hands.

Deuteronomy 2:7 God, we lack nothing.

Deuteronomy 5:2 Lord, You have made an eternal covenant with us.

Deuteronomy 5:28 Lord, You hear our every word and You make them pleasing to Your ears.

Deuteronomy 7:9 God, You are faithful to us and keep Your covenant with us.

Deuteronomy 7:10 God, You judge and destroy the evil we commit. Thank You, God!

Deuteronomy 7:13 Lord, You love us, You bless us, and You multiply us.

Joshua 3:10 You are a living God who lives with us.

Psalms 1:3 You have planted us by streams of living water.

Psalms 3:3 You are our shield, our glory, and You lift our heads to see.

Psalms 4:3 You have set us apart for Yourself.

Psalms 5:7 We come into Your house with the multitude of Your mercy.

Psalms 6:9 You, Lord, hear our supplications and receive our prayers.

Psalms 8:6 You have made us to rule over the works of Your hands.

Psalms 10:16 You are our king forever!

Psalms 10:17 You strengthen our desires.

Psalms 10:17 You strengthen our hearts.

Psalms 10:18 You remove our fears, O Lord.

Psalms 11:1 In Thee, we put our trust.

Psalms 13:5 Our hearts rejoice in Thy salvation.

Psalms 15:4 We who fear Thee are honored to be in Thy presence.

Psalms 16:7 We thank the Lord who gives us counsel.

Psalms 16:8 You are at our right hands, we shall not be shaken.

Psalms 17:15 We behold Your righteous face; we are satisfied.

Psalms 18:2 You are our rock, our fortress, our deliverer.

Psalms 18:3 Lord, we call upon You and praise You.

Psalms 18:19 You have brought us into a large place, You deliver us. You delight in us.

Psalms 18:20 Lord, You reward us according to our righteousness.

Psalms 18:28 You light up our lamps and illuminate our darkness.

Psalms 18:29 By You, O God, we can leap over walls.

Psalms 18:30 God, Your way for us is perfect.

Psalms 18:32 You dress us with strength and make our way blameless.

Psalms 18:35 You give us the shield of salvation and lift us up.

Psalms 18:46 You are our rock; we exalt You by our salvation.

Psalms 18:49 We shall give thanks to Thee and sing praises to Thee.

Psalms 19:7 Your law is perfect, restoring our souls.

Psalms 19:8 Your statutes are right, they rejoice in our hearts.

Psalms 19:8 Your commandments are pure, enlightening our eyes.

Psalms 19:9 Your judgments are true and righteous altogether.

Psalms 19:13 Lord, keep us innocent from great transgressions.

Psalms 19:14 Lord, let the words of our mouths and the meditations of our hearts be acceptable in Thy sight, O Lord, our rock and our redeemer.

Psalms 20:6 Lord, You save Your anointed with Your right hand.

Psalms 20:7 We remember Thy name, O Lord.

Psalms 21:1 How greatly shall we rejoice in Thy salvation!

Psalms 21:2 Lord, You have given us our heart's desire.

Psalms 21:3 You bless us with good things.

Psalms 21:4 You have given us eternal life.

Psalms 21:5 Your glory is revealed in our salvation.

Psalms 21:6 You have blessed us forever; You make us joyful in Your presence.

Psalms 21:13 We sing praise to Thy power.

Psalms 22:1-2 O Lord, how often we believe we are forsaken and alone. Yet, You are our God and we are always in You and You are in us.

Psalms 22:3 Thou, O Lord are Holy.

Psalms 22:4 The Lord delivers us.

Psalms 22:5 We are confused; we cry out and are delivered. We trust and are not disappointed.

Psalms 22:6-8 In the illusion of lies, we are worms, yet You rescue us from these lies and deliver us because You delight in us.

Psalms 22:9-10 You are our life, our breast milk. We have been with Thee since birth.

Psalms 22:19 In times of trouble, You are near and hasten to our assistance.

Psalms 22:20 Lord, You deliver our souls, our lives from evil.

Psalms 22:22 We will praise Thee before everyone.

Psalms 22:23 We are powerless before Thee; we praise Thee and glorify Thee.

Psalms 22:24 When we cry to You in our afflictions, You hear us.

Psalms 22:25 We shall spread Your Word before all the congregation; We will pay homage to You before Your children.

Psalms 22:26 As sinners, we are humbled and nourished by You, Lord, and Your Spirit lives eternally in us.

Psalms 23:1 Lord Jesus, You are our shepherd; we are complete in everything.

Psalms 23:3 Lord, You restore our souls to perfection.

Psalms 23:4 You are with us in this valley of death; we fear no evil because of You; You comfort us with Your staff of truth.

Psalms 23:5 You feed us as we face danger; You anoint us with Your oil of purity; we are blessed with Your plenty.

Psalms 23:6 Your goodness and loving kindness follow us forever.

Psalms 24:1 Lord, we are Yours; the earth is Yours; the Universe is Yours.

Psalms 24:8 You instruct us who are sinners; You are good!

Psalms 25:2 O Lord, we lift our souls up to You; in You we trust.

Psalms 25:3 Lord, we serve You with joy!

Psalms 25:5 As the God of our salvation; lead and teach us.

Psalms 25:9 We humble ourselves before You; teach us Your ways.

Psalms 25:10 All Your paths are mercy and truth.

Psalms 25:12-13 We fear only You; teach us the way that we shall choose that our souls may dwell in peace and our offspring shall inherit eternity.

Psalms 25:14 Your secret is with us who fear You.

Psalms 26:1 We walk in Your integrity, trusting in You for our standing.

Psalms 26:3 Thy loving kindness is before our eyes; we walk in Thy truth.

Psalms 26:8 O Lord, we love the habitation of Thy house where Thy honor dwells.

Psalms 27:1 Lord, You are our light and our salvation; we fear no one. You are the strength of our life.

Psalms 27:10 When we are forsaken, take us unto Thyself.

Psalms 27:14 We will serve You, Lord with courage, and You shall strengthen our hearts.

Psalms 28:7 Lord, You are our strength and shield.

Psalms 29:1 We will praise Thee, O Lord, for Thy Glory and strength.

Psalms 29:4 Your voice is powerful and majestic!

Psalms 29:10 Lord, You sit as King over our floods forever.

Psalms 29:11 Lord, You bless us with Your peace.

Psalms 30:2 Lord, as we have cried unto Thee, we are healed.

Psalms 30:3 Thou hast brought our souls from the grave, hast kept us alive and out of the pit.

Psalms 30:4 We sing praise unto Thee and give thanks to Your Holy Name.

Psalms 30:5 Though Your anger is for a moment, Your favor is eternal.

Psalms 30:11 Thou hast turned our mourning into dancing!

Psalms 30:12 In our glory, we sing praise unto You and give thanks unto Thee forever.

Psalms 31:1 In Thee, O Lord, we have taken refuge, in Thy righteousness deliver us.

Psalms 31:2 Lord, we call unto You to rescue us; You are our strong rock and defense.

Psalms 31:3 Thou art our rock, our fortress; lead us and guide us.

Psalms 31:4 Lord, You have pulled us from the nets by Your great strength.

Psalms 31:14 We trust in Thee, O Lord, Thou art our God!

Psalms 31:19 How great is Thy goodness, O Lord!

Psalms 32:5 We confess our sins unto You, O Lord, Thou dost forgive the guilt of our sin.

Psalms 33:1 We will sing for joy to Thee, O Lord.

Psalms 33:22 Let Thy loving kindness be upon us, O Lord.

Psalms 34:1 We will bless the Lord at all times; our praise of You shall continually be in our mouths.

Psalms 34:8 We will taste and see that the Lord is good!

Psalms 37:4 When we delight ourselves in the Lord; He gives us the desires of our hearts.

Psalms 37:34 When we wait upon the Lord and keep His way; He exalts us to inherit the land.

Psalms 39:1 Lord, we will guard our ways and muzzle our tongues.

Psalms 40:8 We delight to do Thy will, O God, Thy law is within our hearts.

Psalms 41:1 God, we are helpless; deliver us from trouble.

Psalms 42:1 As a deer pants for the water brooks, so our souls thirst for God, for Thee the living God!

Psalms 42:8 The Lord commands His loving kindness in the daytime; His song is with us in the night, and our prayer is to the God of our lives.

Psalms 43:3 O send out Thy light and Thy truth, let them lead us to Thy Holy hill.

Psalms 44:20-21 If we have forgotten the name of our God, or extended our hands to a strange god; God will find this out, for He knows the secrets of our hearts.

Psalms 46:1-2 God, You are our refuge and strength, a very present help in our trouble, we will not fear, though the earth shall change!

Psalms 46:4-7 There is a river whose streams make glad the city of God, God is in the midst of her; the Lord is with us.

Psalms 48:1 Great is the Lord, and greatly to be praised.

Psalms 51:1 Be gracious to us, O God, according to Thy loving-kindness: according to the greatness of Thy compassion blot out our transgressions.

Psalms 51:2 Wash us thoroughly from our iniquities, and cleanse us from our sins.

Psalms 51:3-4 For we know our transgressions, and our sins are ever before us; against Thee, Thee only, we have sinned, and done what is evil in Thy sight.

Psalms 51:10 Create in us clean hearts, O God, and renew stead-fast spirits within us.

Psalms 51:11 Do not cast us away from Thy presence, and do not take Thy Holy Spirit from us.

Psalms 51:12-13 Restore to us the joy of our salvation, and sustain us with willing spirits. Then we will teach transgressors Thy ways, and sinners will be converted to Thee.

Psalms 51:14 Deliver us from blood guiltiness, O God, Thou God of our salvation; then our tongues will joyfully sing of Thy righteousness.

Psalms 54:4 Behold, God is our helper; The Lord is the sustainer of our souls.

Psalms 55:16 We shall call upon God, and the Lord will save us.

Psalms 62:1 Our souls wait in silence for God only; from Him is our salvation.

Psalms 90:1-2 Lord, Thou hast been our dwelling place in all generations. Before the mountains were born, or Thou didst give birth to the Earth and the world, even from everlasting to everlasting, Thou art God.

Psalms 90:12 God, teach us to number our days, that we may present to Thee a heart of wisdom.

Psalms 92:1-2 It is good to give thanks to the Lord, and to sing praises to Thy name, O Most High; to declare Thy loving kindness in the morning, and Thy faithfulness by night.

Psalms 95:1-3 O come, let us sing for joy to the Lord; let us shout joyfully to the rock of our salvation. Let us come before His presence with thanksgiving; let us shout joyfully to Him with psalms.

Psalms 100:1-5 Make a joyful noise unto the Lord, all ye lands. Serve the Lord with gladness: come before His presence with singing. Know ye that the Lord, He is God: it is He that hath made us, and not we ourselves; we are His people, and the sheep of His pasture. Enter into His gates with thanksgiving, and into His courts with praise: be thankful unto Him, and bless His name. For the Lord is good; His mercy is everlasting; and His truth to all generations.

Psalms 103:1-5 Bless the Lord, O our souls; and all that is within us, bless His holy name. Bless the Lord, O our souls, and forget none of His benefits; Who pardons all our iniquities; Who heals all our diseases; Who redeems our lives from the pit; Who crowns us with loving kindness and compassion; Who satisfies our years with good things, so that our youth is renewed like the eagles.

Psalms 121:1-4 We will lift up our eyes to the mountains; from whence shall our help come? Our help comes from the Lord, who made heaven and earth. He will not allow our feet to slip; He who keeps us will neither slumber nor sleep.

Psalms 121:5-8 The Lord is our keeper; the Lord is our shade on our right hands. The sun will not smite us by day, nor the moon by night. The Lord will protect us from all evil; He will keep our soul. The Lord will guard our going out and our coming in from this time forth and forevermore.

Psalms 133:1 Behold, how good and how pleasant it is for brothers and sisters to dwell together in unity.

Psalms 139:1-4 Lord, Thou hast searched us and known us. Thou knowest our downsitting and our uprising, Thou understandest our thoughts afar off. Thou compassest our paths and our lying down, and art acquainted with all our ways.

Psalms 139:5-6 Thou hast beset us behind and before, and laid Thine hand upon us. Such knowledge is too wonderful for us; it is high, we cannot attain unto it.

Psalms 139:17-18 How precious also are Thy thoughts unto us, O God! How great is the sum of them! If we should count them, they are more in number than the sand: when we awake, we are still with Thee.

Psalms 139:23-24 Search us, O God, and know our heart: try us, and know our thoughts: And see if there be any wicked way in us, and lead us in the way everlasting.

Psalms 150:1-2 Praise ye the Lord. Praise God in His sanctuary: praise Him in the firmament of His power. Praise Him for His mighty acts: praise Him according to His excellent greatness.

Psalms 150:3-4 Praise the Lord with the sound of trumpets: praise Him with the psaltery and harp. Praise Him with the timbrel and dance: praise Him with stringed instruments and organs.

Psalms 150:5-6 Praise Him upon the loud cymbals: praise Him upon the high sounding cymbals. Let everything that hath breath praise the Lord. Praise ye the Lord!

Ecclesiastes 3:14 We know that whatsoever God doeth, it shall be forever: nothing can be put to it, nor anything taken from it: and God doeth it, that men shall fear before Him.

Matthew 5:13 We are the salt of the earth.

Matthew 5:14 We are the light of the world.

Matthew 7:24 Everyone who hears these words of mine and acts upon them, may be compared to a wise man.

Matthew 27:37 This is Jesus the King of the Jews.

Mark 11:23-24 What we say in faith without doubt we get.

Luke 11:9-10 We ask and we receive: we seek and we find; we knock and the door is opened unto us.

John 3:36 We have eternal life if we believe in Jesus.

John 5:24 Truly, truly, I say unto you, they who hear my word, and believe Him who sent me, has eternal life. John 6:35 Jesus said, I am the bread of life; you who come to me shall not hunger, and you who believe in me shall never thirst.

John 7:37 If anyone is thirsty, let that one come to me and drink.

John 7:38 Whoever believes in Jesus, from his innermost being shall flow rivers of living water.

John 14:14 If we ask anything in Jesus' name, He will do it.

John 14:15 If we love Jesus, we will keep His commandments.

John 14:27 Jesus said, Peace I leave with you; My peace I give to you.

John 15:16 Jesus said, we did not choose Him, but He chose us.

John 15:17 Jesus said, this I command you that you love one another.

John 17:13 Jesus said, we have His joy that we may be made full in each other.

John 17:17 We are sanctified in the truth.

John 17:18 We are sent into the world by God.

John 17:22 We have God's glory that we may be one with God.

John 17:23 We are perfected in God's unity.

John 21:19 Jesus said, follow Me!

Romans 1:6 We are the called of Jesus Christ.

Romans 1:7 We are beloved of God and called saints.

Romans 3:19 We are all accountable to God.

Romans 5:1 We have peace with God through Jesus Christ.

Romans 5:2 We have grace through Christ.

Romans 5:3-4 We exalt in our tribulations, knowing that they bring about perseverance; and perseverance, proven character; and proven character, hope.

Romans 5:6 For while we were helpless, at the right time Christ died for us.

Romans 5:10 For while we were enemies, we were reconciled to God through Jesus Christ.

Romans 5:17-18 We thank God that we have now become slaves to righteousness.

Romans 5:22 We, having been freed from sin and enslaved to God, we receive sanctification and the outcome is eternal life.

Romans 5:23 The free gift of God is eternal life in Christ Jesus our Lord.

Romans 6:3 We who have been baptized into Christ Jesus have been baptized into His death.

Romans 6:8 We who have died with Christ, also live.

Romans 8:1 We who are in Christ Jesus are under no condemnation.

Romans 8:2 We are set free from sin and death by the law of the Spirit of life in Christ Jesus.

Romans 8:11 We have life in our mortal bodies through His Spirit which indwells us.

Romans 8:16 We are children of God.

Romans 8:17 We are heirs of God and fellow heirs with Christ.

Romans 8:28 We know that God causes all things to work together for good to those who love God, to those who are called according to His purpose.

Romans 8:29-30 God forknew us, He predestined us to become conformed to the image of His Son, that He might be the the first-born among many of us; and whom God pre-destined, these He called, these He also justified; and whom He justified, these He also glorified.

Romans 8:35 Who shall separate us from the love of Christ?

Romans 8:38-39 For we are convinced that neither death, nor life, nor angels, nor principalities, nor things present, nor things to come, nor powers, nor height, nor depth, nor any other created thing, shall be able to separate us from the love of God, which is in Christ.

Romans 12:3 God has allotted to each of us a measure of faith.

Romans 12:6 May each of us exercise our faith according to the measure proportioned to us.

Romans 14:7-8 For we do not live unto ourselves or die to ourselves, for if we live, we live to the Lord, or if we die, we die for the Lord; we are the Lord's.

Romans 14:22 Happy are we who do not condemn ourselves.

Romans 15:13 May the God of hope fill us with all joy and peace.

Spiritual living has caused me to radically adjust my prayer life. I decided that if God's will is always done, maybe I should cease requesting His will be done. Maybe I should begin thanking God for the blessing of His will being completed. I ask God to infuse me with the reality of being awake to enjoy His will being done and to serve Him as I am blessed by it. I know that I can best demonstrate God's truth in me by actively forcing my physical to conform to the beauty planted in my soul. I find that this mode of praying thankfully is most important when I feel especially challenged. This can happen in an instant, especially when one works in a stressful or negative environment.

Over the past eighteen years as a prison chaplain I have learned to force myself to thank God for going before me to open opportunities of service and challenge. Frequently challenges can come from the men incarcerated there; however, it most often is encountered in staff-to-staff conflicts and in staff-to-rules conflicts. Recently, I was praying quietly in my office during the period when no inmates were around. Two staff members observed me from a distance of at least fifty feet and believed I was sleeping. They reported this to the administration, and I was reprimanded.

This incident has reminded me of the lesson Jesus taught us in His ministry. That lesson is that our best intentions and finest examples of Sabbath living often will confuse those around us. We should not be surprised or angered by another's misunderstanding. We need to use this as an opportunity to live as Christ has taught us. We are called to live the joy of our salvation with the excitement of a child of God. Paul clearly defines this issue in Romans 14:13ff. Here he cautions us to refrain from putting stumbling blocks in others' way. Instead we are to use the problems we experience as opportunities to love our brothers.

I need to view my own sorrow or distress as minimal compared to the sorrow or distress of inmates as they receive news of family illnesses and deaths. Often the news comes in a blatant and unexpected manner and at a particularly vulnerable moment. Only the most ignorant or callous person would not want to reach out and lend a shoulder. However, pain of this kind is usually so deep that no pick or shovel could reach it. It is at these moments that one does best just to sit with the man and allow him to vent his feelings of sorrow and sadness.

At times such as this I search for questions to ask that will allow the sorrowing one to tell me his story of the relationship. In between his answers, I give time for any thoughts that may need to be expressed. Do I ever think that I help? I have never conceived that my being there is of any more help than if I were a fellow pilgrim who has a common attachment to life. I take no credit for his successful walk through the valley. I believe he already knows that God is his ultimate help and guide. We eventually pray together and usually exchange a hug. I want him to know that love is more powerful than death, but no lecture or sermon is ever delivered.

In order to prepare ourselves for the demanding responsibilities that both Jane and I shall be assuming each day, we begin with prayer. At breakfast each morning as Jane and I pray, I thank God for the day, for the food, for our love, for the tasks before us, and for His guidance as we are about these tasks. I want to remind us that we are God's children along with all his other children. I also need to affirm that God has provided us with everything that we have need of during this day. Consequently, as we climb the mountains or swim the rivers, we lack nothing.

In 1984, Jane and I were in California at a seminar. While on a brief recess, we met a man who told us about his financial giving to God. He said that his life had been a shambles until someone told him about tithing. He began to do so and his life immediately changed for the better; consequently, he decided that if ten percent would improve his life that much, he would give twenty percent. His life improved even more and he became even richer, so he gave thirty, forty, fifty, sixty, seventy, eighty percent. At that time of the seminar, he was giving ninety percent of his income to his church for the Lord. This gentleman said that the next step was for him to give all he received to God and see if life could be any more sublime.

This wonderful man's story was a guilt trip for me until I understood the fallacy that lay at the heart of it. God has given us one hundred percent of what we need for our lives. My giving, your giving, or this man's giving does not trigger more giving on God's part. What was happening in this man's life was more focus and dedication on his part. The more that I give of myself to the Master, the more I focus on what I have been given and honor these blessings.

At this point, I feel the need to explain how I attempt to be in as constant an awareness of God working in my life as possible. Each morning, I encourage men to come to my office for a one-hour Bible study. Usually those who come bring their Bibles or I supply them with whatever translation they wish to use. Many of them have Bible translations that they have received from their religious community or from other groups they have contacted.

I am comfortable using almost any translation of the Bible; however, I refrain from using paraphrased Bibles or Bibles with added commentaries of wise men. These have proven to be stultifying and unproductive in my daily journey to discover how great a God we worship. I prefer using the *New American Standard Bible* along with the 1611 version of the *King James Bible*. I use the latter because it is the one I grew up reading and memorizing. I admit that I love its wonderful phrasing. I am well aware of the archaic language and enjoy comparing it to The New American Standard.

I use the *Strong's Exhaustive Concordance of the Bible* as a cross-reference for words I desire to study in relation to their contextual use. I am aware that Strong's is theologically oriented to fundamentalistic Christianity; however, I still find it valuable as a resource tool. This concordance is available in both the *King James English* and in the *English of the New International Version of the Bible*. I prefer the former because I am comfortable with the 1611 language and its often archaic usage.

Before we begin our Bible study, I invite someone to pray whatever prayer he desires. As we explore the Bible, we progress best by reading it aloud a verse at a time. I believe that this is best done with more than one person present. This way one person can read while the others listen, and each person gets an opportunity to read aloud. After the chapter is read, it may be discussed in any manner; however, our best learning is done when we eventually force ourselves to interpret it in the spiritual context with a singular emphasis upon our individual growth need. When in a group, I allow the other participants to choose any book of the Bible. Then we systematically read it from beginning to end, studying only one chapter in any one session. In doing this I have found that every chapter is full of God's spiritual truth.

I have found that Leviticus, the books of the Kings, and the Chronicles are the least productive because they stretch my ability to gain spiritual guidance and meaningful progression. I personally view them as attempts by their authors to cause me to search for a pillow. (God, please forgive me, for I know that You meant me to cherish these as I do the other wonderful gifts You have given.)

For me, reading in the spiritual can best be described as imaging myself as having only a spirit and no physical body. I am residing in God's spiritual hands, completely free from sin due to the Christ-God, and ready to receive God's truth. Being free from the physical means that I desire to perceive no ethnic bias, no sexual bias, no age bias, no monetary bias, or any preferential advantage of any kind. My brothers and sisters and I are made perfect children of and by God.

* * *

If I were you at this time, I would have more questions than answers on my mind. I would question the simplicity of Christocentric truth and especially Sabbath living within this truth. I would ask, "Isn't all this belief that everyone has all the truth that they need for righteous living a fallacy in light of the evil one sees displayed every day?" My answer would be, "For you to acknowledge that we, as God's children, commit evil against ourselves and others only proves the point that we have free choices that we can make. We are not captive souls of an almighty deity who pulls the strings causing us to operate in an expected manner. We are benefitted by a compassionate God who cleanses us from our evil. This is our opportunity to choose to live in the Sabbath, having the judgment of God and the sacrifice of God to condemn us and return us to the possibility of our choosing the Sabbath rather than living in our imaginary six days."

Another question that I have often been asked is, "What happens when we are no longer living in the physical?" This is an easy one. We are so convinced that we are physical beings that we define all our existence in these terms. We date our birth and the date we were created within nine months of each other. As long as we are so imprisoned, we will propose false answers to all our questions. We can begin to solve this quandary by looking to the heavens on a clear night and imagining how many other earths there are in the universe. Then, imagine there is someone a hundred million light years away who is looking for us and possibly asking the same questions. They and we need to cast off the physical and find unity in our spiritual togetherness. The physical always will be an important part of our lives, yet we need to celebrate the freedom casting it off brings and rejoice in it.

I close this chapter with a few words I but believe are fitting here. They come from the pen of my mentor, Dr. Loyal Morris Thompson:

My first hours with a new lens after the operation for cataracts.

I see my wife clearly and she is as tall as she wishes to be but alas the proportion adheres in another direction. I see clearly but it's a wacky world. I reach for a chair and its not there. When I walk, I reel like a drunken sailor. The wash bowl in the bathroom looked so big I almost thought it was the bath tub but it was so high in my sight I knew I could never get up to it. The neighbors' houses seem so close they only look a step away. Well that is enough discoveries for this time. I'm going to keep my wife, bless her whatever proportion she assumes. And I say from the heart, Bless God that He has led me into the light again. And grateful thanks to God for the surgeon whose knowledge and skill under the guidance of God who opened my eye to the light and made possible my journey in the loveliness of God's world of reality again. I said above I was going to keep my wife. That is speaking mildly for she has faithfully led me through the dark days and patiently ministered to my every need. Who could forget this devoted labor of love? (Written Saturday, September 20, 1958 upon his first seeing.)

I also include one of the many poems Dr. Thompson wrote.

The Strong Right Arm of God—
I saw it through a mist of snow
It cheered me so when faith burned low.

The Strong Right Arm of God—
It slipped beneath a Manger-Bed
Where Baby Jesus laid His head.

The Strong Right Arm of God—
So strong so tender it would bear
The whole wide-world within its care.

A sanctuary formed for you
Where aspiration flames anew
In the Strong Right Arm of God!

I know that you already have many letters, poems, essays, and other beautifully written passages that will inspire and comfort you as you choose to live in the Sabbath. God bless you and I'll see you soon! Phil

CHAPTER 6
"The Starting Point"

"The Starting Point" is presented in dialogue format. I have purposefully chosen this in an attempt to demonstrate Christocentric theology in an alternate and possibly clearer manner since this theology has not been previously expounded. I also have attempted to portray this theology in this style so that it lends itself to a play production format or to facilitate it being read aloud in a group setting.

Several Christocentric principles have been illustrated in this play using biblical stories, references, healings of Jesus and His parables. This has been done to validate the coherence and truth of this theology.

Cast of Characters

Interpreter
Phil
God
Michael
Angels
Adam
Animals
Eve
Serpent
Seed
Birds
Rock One
Rock Two
Rock Three
Rock Four
Rock Five

Moses
Hezekiah
Thorns & Thistles
Calach
Yaab
Jesus
Crowd
Pharisees
Innkeeper
Ayin
Shimrayth (Holy Spirit)
Telach
Louis

(SONG 1: OVERTURE)

GOD: (walks on stage, points to Phil and puts him to sleep, walks to the front of the stage, and begins talking to the audience)

Hello, how are you? I already know because I am God and I know what you are thinking. You doubt who I am because you do not expect me to look like this. Well, I Am who I Am, and I appear any way I want to appear. You will just have to adjust your ideas of who I Am.

Today, I am here to get this young man started in doing the tasks that I have called him to do. You are invited to watch. Later, I will come and assist you in getting started. Some of you have been procrastinating far too long.

(God walks toward Phil and awakens him.)

PHIL: As I begin this chapter, I better pray that God will make this time fruitful. Our Father, who art in heaven, hallowed be Thy name. Thy kingdom come, Thy will be done...

GOD: Hello, kid.

PHIL: Kid? Who are you and who are you calling "kid"?

GOD: I Am who I Am! I heard you praying and wondered if you knew to whom you were praying and if you believed in the message you were praying, or were you doing it to make someone else think you are so very holy?

PHIL: Are you really God?!!!!! Are you talking to me?!!!!! I have heard that you still do this and I even remember you talking to me when I was nine years old, but I didn't think that you did it to 62-year-old men, especially not to me.

GOD: Kid, now you know that I even talk to you. By the way, sixty-two isn't so old. Look up the ages of some of the other people I talk with on a regular basis. But enough of this chatter. I have noticed that you have been writing about me and I decided to have some direct input into this book. Don't get excited. I don't care if you publish it or make some money from it; I just want my children to understand a little more about how they are to live eternally.

PHIL: God, I am so unworthy. Why don't you choose someone else?

GOD: Don't be so self-righteous. You are not the one who makes yourself righteous. I am!!!!! If I choose to speak to you now, I am going to speak through you! You do not have to worry about who gets the credit, I'll take care of that issue. Do you know that I have given you life and have placed before you choices?

PHIL: Yes, God.

GOD: Are you also aware that I have instructed you to relate to me spiritually and to apply my teachings to yourself spiritually prior to disciplining your physical self? If you are so knowledgeable, why are you so seldom following my teachings?

PHIL: I confess that I am knowledgeable of your teachings and that I am constantly violating them. Father, please help me!

GOD: Before I can help you, I want you to review the ten guidelines which I have given you. You call them the Ten Commandments. These are necessary requisites for you to successfully participate in eternal living. You must assess each of them spiritually in order to understand their meanings.

PHIL: OK! Here goes. First…

(SONG 2: YOU ARE)

You are our God, who created us, saved us,
And You are the everlasting one!
You are the source of all our goodness,
You are the fullness of our lives.
You are our everlasting Bread.

We live within Your bounty
We reside within Your Sabbath, oh Lord.
We see You as you show yourself to us.
We're here to worship and adore You forever.

For You are our Alpha and Omega,
Our father, our mother, and friend.
Like trees planted by streams of living water,
You nourish and fill us with the strength of life.

As a father lifts his wounded sons and daughters
So You rescue us from violence,
And Your tender love caresses us,
As our mother, You gave us life,
We have been with Thee since birth.

You are our breast milk, As You hold us to Your breast.
You gave us Jesus who calls us His friend,
Yet, our love is weak and faint and we sinners be
Who have placed Him on the cross, as a murderer.
We have stolen, killed, and pillaged what was not ours.

Please tear the scales of sin from off our souls,
For we desire those peaceful days we once enjoyed
When we followed the Lamb so fair.

If this be the ten rules You have impressed on our hearts;
May I never stray from living them each day.

Father, how did I do? I'm sorry that I couldn't recite them as You wrote them.

GOD: I will tell you later after your examination. Now, do you know where you are?

PHIL: Yes, I am now living on Earth. It is a planet that circles around the sun once each year and occupies space in the solar system. It is a small part of what we call the Universe and...

GOD: Kid, I do not need a lecture on the Earth, the solar system, or the universe. I now understand that you have forgotten that you got to this place you call Earth by choosing to enter a manufacturing plant that produced a spacesuit for you and subsequently deposited you on Spaceship Earth. From now on you are a cadet astronaut living for a time on this spaceship. You may refer to me as the Captain, or as God, or as Jesus Christ, or as the Holy Spirit. Remember, I Am the same yesterday, today, and tomorrow.

PHIL: Wow! This is going to be quite an adventure. I'm ready! Let's go flying! I'm glad I chose this spacesuit because things are really getting interesting.

GOD: I know that you think that you chose your spacesuit. However, before you become too exuberant, I ask you to examine how often you have wished for a taller one, a more handsome one, a more athletic one, and especially one without red hair. Well, I took care of the red hair; you will just have to take good care of the rest of your suit yourself. By the way, you did not choose your spacesuit. I chose yours as I chose Adam's, Eve's, Noah's, Moses', Jeremiah's, and I even chose the one that I wore which you call Jesus Christ.

Now, I want you to meet someone whom you met when he came to Jacksonville Correctional Center as an inmate. Listen and learn from him.

MICHAEL: Hi, I'm Michael. When I saw you last, I was in prison for my eighth time. I knew you wouldn't recognize me until I reintroduced myself to you.

PHIL: Michael, I didn't expect to see you. I thought that you had moved to another part of the country. How are you? How did you get here? Are you in prison again?

MICHAEL: I'm fine, and, no, I'm not in prison again. You see me only because God brought me back to talk with you. I am no longer living on Spaceship Earth. However, before I left, I learned the meaning of "Doing His Will," and God wants me to help you.

PHIL: I can't understand why God would tell you such a thing. I have been serving Him for the past forty-plus years as a minister, which includes the last sixteen as a chaplain. What could you possibly teach me that I don't already know?

MICHAEL: God wants me to explain to you how I have lived my life denying His participation and the lessons that I have learned from experiencing continuous hardships and grief until I came to recognize God as the supplier of all my needs.

PHIL: I can't believe that God would send you, a convicted criminal, to tell me these things. After all, I have given my life to helping men and women find God. Have I been a failure in all of my ministry?

MICHAEL: Shazam, you just hit the nail on the head! Have you ever read Psalm 24? In it God tells us to examine our lives and every other person's life with a clean heart. Are you able to listen to me as a child of God or as a felon?

PHIL: You got me there. I will try to listen to you and not judge you. Please go on.

MICHAEL: I grew up in and out of trouble from the time I was able to crawl. By age eight, I was sent to my first youth camp. When I wasn't confined in a youth center, I was either a runner for a drug pusher or was at home getting a beating from my drunken father. I didn't do well in school; either I was suspended or I was skipping.

PHIL: That's too, too bad, but how does that concern me? Tell me what God wants me to know!

MICHAEL: You really are impatient. I used to think you were a good listener. Do you think you could just listen and not interrupt so often?

PHIL: I will if you get on with it! I've heard these stories so often, they are boring.

MICHAEL: Boring is as boring does. Maybe you are sleepwalking through your life as a cadet on planet Earth. Anyway, I will ignore your insolence and tell you what God brought me here to tell you.

By the time I hit Jacksonville and saw you for the first time, I was on my sixth bit. I liked you from the start because you gave me a Bible and some birthday cards to send to my daughter. You also invited me to go to Bible studies and to church. I attended some of your Bible studies, but felt somewhat like you were throwing our need to become Christians in order to go to heaven out the window, so I stopped coming.

By the time I began my eighth bit and my third in Jacksonville, I had spent more time in prison than I had lived on the streets or, as you say, in the free world. The roads I had walked were like rivers at flood stage running into places that they didn't belong. I wanted to get caught in the wrong place at the wrong time and get shot and killed. However, that never happened. Oh, yes, I was shot at many times, but instead of stopping a bullet, I ran and hid.

I was in people's houses stealing TV's, radios, silverware, jewelry, and any money I could find. I walked alleys breaking into garages stealing tools, tires, lawnmowers, and even snow blowers. Can you imagine trying to fence a snow blower when the weather is a hundred degrees in the summer? All I wanted was to get money for my drugs.

PHIL: As I remember, you used cocaine, didn't you?

MICHAEL: By then, I would use almost anything, but I preferred cocaine. When I got busted on that last bit, I was too ashamed to come to your office even to get cards. I took the job in dietary and two days later got mad at another inmate and threw a pan at him. I got thrown into Seg, which was where you first saw me. You didn't even recognize me when I asked you for a Bible.

PHIL: I recognized you, I just couldn't remember your name, and I didn't want to admit that my mind was going fast. Sometimes I can't even remember my own. Please go on.

MICHAEL: When I got the Bible, I decided to read the Twenty-third Psalm. When I finished it, I left the Bible open to think about its meaning. I glanced down at the Psalm again and noticed the fourth verse of Chapter 24, which seemed to be shouting to me to study. I thought of my lifelong confusion and remembered the story of the demon-possessed man Jesus told about, who was tied to the tombs. I looked around and decided that I was as bad off as that guy was. For the first time in my life, I understood that I had been living among the tombs of life and Jesus had been telling me to listen to His voice and follow Him. I had been taking small steps through that minefield with His guidance. I was a survivor, but only with the help of God's salvation.

PHIL: Are you saying that Jesus was in the tombs? Was Jesus in Seg with you? What do you mean?

MICHAEL: That's right, Jesus was in everything. However, everything was not Jesus. All the signs and symbols that had been in my life were choices that God was giving me to honor Him. My problem was in not choosing to serve God in each of the choices. Jesus was always present resurrecting me for another opportunity to choose again. I figured out while sitting in that cell that Jesus resurrected me from my bad decisions at least twenty-three hundred times.

PHIL: Do you mean that all the choices were given to you by God and you misused or misunderstood the gifts that God was giving you, and harmed yourself and others by what you did?

MICHAEL: That's correct. Boy, did I spend the rest of my time while in Seg on my knees asking God to help me figure out a way to serve Him in every choice I received from then on. I also thanked God for never giving up on me and for saving me from myself. I prayed that everyone that I had harmed had insight to accept the healing God gave him or her. Finally, I pledged myself to always keep a clear spirit and mind all the remaining days I had on Earth.

PHIL: Wow! If that had been me, I would have spent the rest of my Earthly life in Seg. What did the committee do to you when they heard your discipline ticket?

MICHAEL: You won't believe this, but when I went before the captain and told him what I had experienced in that cell, and that I wouldn't mind if I could spend a few more days to finish my counting, he looked at me like lightning had struck him. I was sent back to my cell without being told what was going to happen to me. Two hours later, I was sent back to my housing unit.

PHIL: What happened to you after you got out of prison?

MICHAEL: I was released in early summer and took the first job that I could find. In the evenings, I would walk the streets where I had done most of my crimes. I went up to every house that had a lawn that needed mowing and volunteered to mow the grass. Many refused my offer, but for those who accepted, I mowed, trimmed, and edged. They tried to pay me, and I told them to give the money to their favorite charity. Many times they forced money into my pockets. I bought my own lawnmower and continued to serve God. Soon, I began to do this full-time. I even cleaned their walks in the wintertime. Two years after my release, I was mowing a lawn when a car passed me at a high rate of speed, a shot rang out, and I was hit in the head and died instantly. Now, I am here talking to you.

PHIL: You have one fantastic story! Maybe I now understand what God means when He is doing His will in me, and maybe I'll accept the choices that I have as being God's opportunity for me to serve Him. I wonder how many times Jesus has resurrected me. Goodbye, Michael, and thank you.

ANGELS: (SONG 3: SING PRAISE)

Sing praise to God who reigns above
the God of all creation,
the God of power, the God of love,
the God of our salvation;
with healing balm my soul fills,

and every faithless murmur stills:
to God all praise and glory.

The Lord is never far away,
but, through all grief distressing,
an ever-present help and stay,
our peace and blessing;
as with a mother's tender hand,
he leads his own, his chosen band

Thus all my gladsome way along
I sing aloud thy praises,
that men may hear the grateful song
my voice unwearied raises;
be joyful in the Lord, my heart;
soul and body bear your part:
to God all praise and glory.
Sing praise to God who reigns above.
(J. J.. Schutz, 1640-90)

PHIL: Give us this day our daily bread…

GOD: Kid, why are you praying for something that I have already given you, or are you just praying that magic prayer again because you do not know who I am? You remind me of someone who, after being out on trepid seas for a long time anchored his boat to what seemed like a safe and large island, only to find to his great surprise that it was a great beast of the sea, which woke up and went charging off with him, boat and all, across the tossing ocean. Where have you put your anchor as you ask for your daily bread?

PHIL: I don't know what I am praying to receive. I think that I want peace, health, goodness, happiness, plenty, and everything wonderful.

GOD: I will introduce you to someone you may have heard of and read about, maybe he can help you to focus a little better on how you can look to me for your specific needs and appreciate what you receive. Adam, will you come here? I want you to meet this new kid who calls himself Phil. Will you tell him how you learned that I fill all your needs?

ADAM: Of course. I'll be glad to serve you, God! I'll help this new cadet understand what it means to live here on this ship. (Adam looks at Phil while God vanishes from the scene.) Hello, Phil. I hear that you are new to this spaceship. Welcome aboard!

PHIL: Are you really The Adam, I mean, THE ADAM AND EVE from the Bible?

ADAM: You look a little startled! Didn't you think that I would still be around? Did you think that just because Eve and I died and were transported by God to the farm to face tough conditions meant that we ceased to be?

PHIL: I didn't mean to stare and appear afraid of you, but you look so different from what I expected. You look so much like ME! You don't look evil.

ADAM: Most people think of me as evil and cowardly for being the first one that was used to illustrate the tasks required of us while living as astronaut on Spaceship Earth. However, you should know that God is my Savior as well as yours.

PHIL: (Leaning up close to Adam so no one else can hear, Phil whispers in Adam's ear.) Are we all cursed? Is this Hell? Are we in Eternal Punishment?

ADAM: I will leave that up to you to answer. I will tell you that many cadets have come here and spent much of their early time cursing me for every problem they have, for every failure they experience, for every disease they or their junior cadets bear, and for every fight they have with other astronauts. You have to decide how you are going to accommodate yourself while here on the spaceship. Now, I must do as God instructed me. Please feel free to ask any questions as I explain how I learned to accept God's gifts and to worship Him for these gifts.

PHIL: I will do my best to listen to you and not drift off into the hideous pictures I have always had of you. Please proceed. I'll just sit over here.

(Phil moves to the side and slowly disappears from view while Adam begins to explain and demonstrate his indoctrination as a cadet.)

ADAM: OK, OK, kid. I guess you have a right to your prejudices. Now here are the facts. After I hid from God and tried to blame Eve for my decision, I was sent to the farm to work in the fields cultivating them. As I arrived, I saw that these fields were covered with rocks, thorns, briars, and thistles, and it even appeared that the soil was rock hard because it had never been cultivated.

I accepted that this was to be my eternal punishment for disobeying God. The first thing I did was to find a place for Eve and me to stay at night. Then I decided to find a way to get to the fields. The first way that I took was a wide road that drew me down it for many miles. Just as I thought that the fields were in sight, I dropped into a deep hole and slid for what seemed like hours, landing in a deep swamp. I was sure I would drown, but I grabbed onto a big log. The log began to snap at me with its huge teeth.

I jumped as I had never jumped before, and this great monster just missed taking the leg of my spacesuit off. When I jumped, I caught a vine that allowed me to climb out of that hole. As I shimmied up, I heard the alligator and all the other animals screaming in wild song.

ANIMALS: (SONG 4: ANIMALS IN EDEN)
We will eat you. We will scare you.
We will have you for our meal!
We will follow , we will haunt you
For you are our food!
You cannot escape our table.
You cannot leave us for long
For we are your worst fear!
We will eat you alive, alive, alive, alive.
Breakfast, lunch, and dinner.
We will eat you alive!

ADAM:
I cried out to the Lord:
Hear my prayer, O Lord.
Give ear to my supplications!
The enemy is persecuting my soul;

160

He is crushing my life to the ground;
He has made me dwell in dark places,
Like those who have been dead.
My soul is overwhelmed within me.
I stretch out my hands to Thee!

I seemed to be lifted up out of that death trap and knelt down on the ground
to thank the Lord for my salvation. I returned to our home on the wide road
that led to destruction and decided that there must be another way to the
fields.

EVE: Adam, what has happened to you? Are you hurt? You are bleeding
from your arms and legs, your hands have such large sores on them. Adam,
Adam, speak to me!!!

ADAM: I could barely crawl into the yard, I heard Eve but could not
answer. I could only cry, for my wounds were great and my fear was even
greater. Eve took leaves and gently washed my wounds. She placed my head
into her lap and sang to me.

EVE: Like summer seas that leave with silent tides a lonely shore,
Like whispering winds that stir the tops of forest trees,
Like a still small voice calling us in the night,
Like a child's hand that feels about a fast closed door;
Gentle, unnoticed and oft in vain;
So is Thy coming, O Lord.

Like ships storm-tossed,
Like starving souls seeking bread,
Like wanderers begging refuge from the whelming night,
Prodigals seeking the Father's home when all is spent;
Welcomed at the door, arms outstretched in forgiving love.
So is our coming to Thee, O God.
So is our coming to Thee.

Like flowers uplifted to the sun,
Like trees that bend before the storm,
Like sleeping seas that mirror cloudless skies,

Like a harp to the hand, like an echo to a cry,
With all our stubbornness, failure, and sin;
We come to Thee, O Lord.

ADAM: We fell asleep in each others arms. Asleep under the tall trees, under the night sky. Tomorrow is another day to find the fields to cultivate.

PHIL: Adam, what happened to you? You look like you were in a fight with a giant. Who won the battle?

ADAM: I could explain it to you. However, let's just say that I survived a rough day yesterday. I can also tell you that the Lord supplied my needs yesterday and that even though I was unable to know what these needs were prior to the day and somewhat unable to accept them today, yet I submit my life to God.

PHIL: Please explain. I do not have the slightest understanding of what you have just said.

ADAM: Well, I am a bit new to this explaining business, but I can best describe it as "He who supplies seed to the sower and bread for food…harvest for…righteousness." This will be clearer to you later because you probably cannot conceive that God can supply a road to walk that involves extreme suffering. You may remember that God told all of us that we have to pick up our cross and follow Him. This is part of the Lord teaching me His paths and leading me into areas that I may understand His truth. When I almost had my spacesuit eaten, I called upon the Lord, and He brought me out of the pit. I now know how much attraction the wide and easy road can hold.

PHIL: I guess that this might be what God means when He tells me that I will be sitting in the company of evil doers and will have to shrink from evil schemes. I thought that living in this spacesuit would be easy.

ADAM: I suggest that you lose "easy" from your vocabulary. Watch closely now as I explain what happened next as I lived on the farm.

(Phil moves to the side and Adam continues his story.)

When I awoke the next morning, I was very sore. However, I knew that for us to survive, we must have food. My responsibility was to clear the ground, cultivate it, and plant it. So, I started to find another path that would lead me to the fields.

EVE: Adam, please be careful! I need you, and I worry about you.

ADAM: Having faced the wild beasts in the pit and survived, I told myself that I could overcome anything that I might face on this new path.

INTERPRETER: Little did Adam know that his pride and arrogance was already taking hold of his decision making.

ADAM: After considerable searching, I found a narrow path that wound along a beautiful stream. I felt very happy even though my cuts and bruises still bothered me. I knew that the fields would have water to grow the crops that I would plant with the seed that God promised He would supply. As I began walking on this narrow road to my fields, I noticed seeds scattered along this road and I wondered how they got there. It seemed such a waste on the sower's part to be so careless, but I was more concerned with getting to my own work. I reached down and picked up a large club. "Why am I picking this up?" I asked myself. I couldn't figure it out, but I held onto it anyway.

SERPENT: I had just gone for a swim in the stream and was now lying on the narrow path beside the stream. I was looking forward to sunning myself, but I was a little disturbed that all these seeds were sticking to my skin. I didn't know who spilled them, but I did know that they were sticking to me and bothering me. Oh well, I guess that I could just have to endure some discomfort.

ADAM: The sky was so blue and beautiful that I could not keep my gaze off it. Kaboom, my feet went right out from under me, and I felt like I had landed on a giant log. Before I could recover, that log started to attack me. It wound around me like a huge vine. I thought that I was going to have my spacesuit crushed. I dropped the club that I was carrying and felt helpless. I cried out, "Lord, hasten to me! Give ear to my voice…do not leave me defenseless." Just then a great vice clamped onto my heel. I not only felt as though I was being crushed, I also felt that my spacesuit foot was being ripped from the rest of me. I called out again, "O Lord, from the snare of this that would do iniquity upon me, let the wicked fall unto its net and release me!"

SEED: We are Adam's salvation; We shall save him who calls upon us who have been placed here to sacrifice ourselves for this child of ours. Come let us strive together to avail the stick that was placed for Adam to pick up and that he now has dropped, so that he may use it as it is intended.

ADAM: I felt the club in my hand again, and with one last bit of my waning strength, I swung it wildly, hitting the serpent on the head. Immediately, I was released from this death trap.

INTERPRETER: Adam and the serpent lay as if dead for a long time. Then, as they revived, they looked at each other.

SERPENT: Wow! Do I ever have a splitting headache! Who are you, and why did you step on me? And what possessed you to hit me so hard over the head with that club in your hand?

ADAM: Who are you and why were you lying in the road where I was walking so that I fell on top of you? Boy, do I hurt! You almost ruined my spacesuit! Why did you try to bite off my foot?

INTERPRETER: They both stared at each other, then both broke out in the most awful scream and laugh mixed that you could ever imagine because they both remembered that fateful day when God told them that "He shall bruise you on the head, And you shall bruise him on the heel."

PHIL: That's bizarre! Do you mean that you and a serpent laid on the ground and talked with each other?

ADAM: That may be strange to you, yet at the time it seemed very much the thing to do. What bothers me about the whole episode is that I never once recognized that my salvation was in God placing the log in my way causing me to consider picking it up and in God sacrificing His seed to enable me to pick up the club after I had dropped it. I never did thank God for His saving grace in that whole incident. For this I am very remorseful. I just thought that I was lucky to have the club when I needed it, and I was angry at God for not saving me when I called on Him.

PHIL: You must be joking when you say that God caused you to see the club, that God placed the seed on the path, and that God shoved the club back into your hand. Aren't you?

ADAM: No! I am very serious about this. Salvation is God being God caring for us in the most unusual manner. I am comfortable in saying that God placed Christ in the club, in the seed, and both carried out their sacrificial purposes.

PHIL: You are way, way, way out there! I'm not very sure that I want to hear much more.

ADAM: You said that you would stick around and hear the whole story. Well, why don't you let me continue with it, and then you can decide?

PHIL: Sorry! Go on with your story.

ADAM: I continued along the road and noticed the birds eating the seeds. I heard them singing,

BIRDS: (SONG 5: SONG OF THE BIRDS)
We hear the sounds of woodland music,
Song of the birds and hum of bee;
Soft winds playing in the branches,
Clear brooks purling minstrelsy.

Silent trumpets of the dawning
Sound a mystic reveille!
While a quiet fading splendor
Breathes a psalm at close of day.

As a Finger touches gently
My taut heart sings out lovingly
All my heart is filled with glory,
Blending in God's harmony.

We hear the sounds of woodland music,
Song of the birds and hum of bee;

Soft winds playing in the branches,
Clear brooks purling minstrelsy.

ADAM: By the time I arrived at the fields, I was feeling so much better because of the singing of the forest, the animals, and the wind. I'm glad that I felt better because the process to grow crops was just as the Lord had decreed it to be. Plenty of rocks, thistles, thorns, and even seed, and I quickly observed that the rocks were so plentiful that although the seed sprang forth quickly, it soon died for lack of earth to nourish it. I spent many a day removing the rocks to the edge of the field, thus allowing the seed to grow.

ROCK ONE: Then Jesus was led up by the Spirit into the wilderness to be tempted by the devil. And after He had fasted forty days and forty nights, He became hungry. And the tempter came and said to Him, "If you are the Son of God, command that these stones become bread." But He answered and said, "It is written, Man shall not live on bread alone, but on every word that proceeds out of the mouth of God."

ROCK TWO: "Teacher, rebuke your disciples." And He answered and said, "I tell you if these become silent, the stones will cry out." And when He approached, Jesus saw the city and wept over it.

ROCK THREE: "Therefore everyone who hears these words of Mine, and acts upon them, may be compared to a wise man, who built his house upon the rock. And the rain descended, and the floods came, and the winds blew, and burst against that house; and yet it did not fall, for it had been founded upon the rock."

ROCK FOUR: He said to them, "But who do you say that I am?" And Simon Peter answered and said, "Thou art the Christ, the Son of the living God." And Jesus answered and said unto him, "Blessed are you, Simon Barjona, because flesh and blood did not reveal this to you, but My Father who is in heaven."

ROCK FIVE: "For I do not want you to be unaware, brethren, that our fathers were all under the cloud, and all passed through the sea; and all were baptized into Moses in the cloud and in the sea; and all ate the same spiritual food; and all drank the same spiritual drink, for they were drinking from a spiritual rock which followed them; and the rock was Christ."

ADAM: I lugged so many rocks from that field that I cursed each one personally. I could not understand how God could be so cruel as to hatch ten rocks where I had just removed one. I not only cursed the rocks, I cursed God for creating the rocks. Only when I began to see that God had given me the rocks to build a house for Eve and me did the rocks cease to multiply. I decided that I was a slow learner for I lugged many a thousand rocks.

INTERPRETER: Eve looked at Adam's spacesuit and admired it for the way that it stretched in so many places.

EVE: Adam, you are so very handsome!!!! I love coming here and watching you work to clear the land so that the seed will grow. The house you are building for us is very beautiful! Could you put another window in the bedroom and could you put on a deck so that we can barbecue out when the neighbors come by to eat with us?

ADAM: Eve, I am working as hard as I am able. I am glad that I finally discovered what God wanted me to do with the rocks. I will do as you wish and make those changes, but right now I am so very tired, that I think I will sit down here next to you for a while.

EVE: Yes, my dear do sit for a while, and as you rest I will wash your beautiful body with these soft leaves. I hope they will sooth your sore muscles.
Adam, you are my beloved! Your hair is like gold, pure gold, and your eyes are like doves beside streams of water bathed in milk! Your cheeks are like a bed of balsam, and your lips are lilies dripping with liquid myrrh. Your abdomen is carved ivory inlaid with sapphires. Your legs are pillars of alabaster set on pedestals of pure gold!

ADAM: Eve, I have never heard you speak like that before. I have often watched as you brought my dinner to the field for me to eat. How beautiful you are, my darling! Many a night I have sought you in my dreams as I slept here in the fields after a long day's work. Secretly, I have left my place here and have run to your bed. I have desired you for so long, and yet I was so afraid because I blamed you for our being put in this place. I wondered if you could ever forgive me. Please say that you forgive me!!!!!

EVE: Adam, I forgave you a long time ago. Come with me to the pool, and we shall wash ourselves and bathe ourselves in the spices that grow there.

INTERPRETER: Adam became even more ambitious in his rock carrying as he realized that Eve's body was changing. He soon realized that those changes announced that a baby was to be added to the household and another room needed to be built.

ADAM: With an additional mouth to feed, I got real busy and finished cleaning the field of rocks. I also began…

PHIL: Hold it! Hold It! You are going far too fast for me. Remember you have already gone through this experience and have even had many, many years to observe and interpret what this Spaceship Earth means. I am new and you have not answered many of my questions.

ADAM: I told you to listen carefully and you would be able to learn. Are you so dense that you cannot understand how simple learning to live on Spaceship Earth can be?

PHIL: Right now, the least of my concerns is about your Spaceship Earth! I want some answers to my earlier question. Are we in Hell?

GOD: I'll take it for a little while, Adam. The kid is so distracted that he can't see the nose in front of his face. I'll bring you back to finish your explanation in a little while. Kid, I think that you should talk with the serpent.

PHIL: I'm always getting the royal run-around here. Why can't God answer some questions for Himself? Adam may like talking to the serpent, but I have nothing to say to it, and I refuse to listen to it. What would my friends say if they knew that I was talking to a serpent, anyway? Most of them think that I should be on the funny farm already.

SERPENT: Hi, kid! Hey, come back here. I'm not going to hurt you. I just want to answer some of your most important questions.

(Phil looks out at the serpent from behind a very large leaf and refuses to talk.)

Kid, come out, come out, wherever you are. I promise you that your coming out will be better than my coming to get you.

PHIL: Your promises don't inspire me after what you did to poor Eve. You, you, you mean serpent. Look what you did to Eve. She and Adam were in perfect wholeness. They were able to talk with God. They were able to walk with God in the stillness of the evening. They had God's constant blessing until you entwined yourself in what was strictly their business. You messed everything up, and look how this world is now. We have people hating each other, people killing each other, people dying from disease, and millions upon millions of people in prisons while their families are suffering miserably.

SERPENT: Hold it! Hold it! Pull your pitchfork out of my hide! You certainly have your preconceived ideas about me. Are you always this prejudiced?

PHIL: Prejudiced !!!!!!!!!!!!! I'm not prejudiced, I'm angry!!!!!!! If you think for a moment that you can cool my anger, you have another think coming. I'm going to give you only a brief minute to explain yourself, then I'm out of here.

SERPENT: Sit down on this rock, and I promise to be brief. You can judge for yourself if what I am telling you makes reasonable sense. Just try to be fair. You have only heard the story from those who do not like me. Now you will hear my side. You have called me serpent, do you call me by any other names?

PHIL: One of the names that you are called is snake because you have no legs and crawl along the ground. I don't like snakes, though others do. You are also called the devil or Satan because you are the one who betrays the trust that is placed in you and because you are so evil.

(SONG 6: THE SERPENT IS A SERVANT OF GOD)

Now, you all blamed me when everything went wrong.
Shamed me, hated me, blamed me for your sin.

You called me names, but did you ever ask
Just why God chose me for this task?

The serpent is a servant of God.
I do what God tells me.
Work in mysterious ways for Him
I'm a child of the Lord. Yes, a child of the Lord.

Oh, yes, you saw me as evil and sin.
Blamed me. Hated me. Lay your sins on me.
Every one. Yet in your heart, you knew
That you could choose your way.

Oh, yes, you know that you choose your every move.
Plan it. Make the choice. People choose their path.
Every day. You have the choice
To carve a path that leads to God.

SERPENT: You call ME evil! Have you not heard of all the good that I have done? You ought to talk to Moses and hear his opinion of me. Moses, Moses, where are you?

MOSES:. Here I am, what do you want? Hello, Serpent, glad to see you! Who is this?

SERPENT: Just a new space cadet. Please tell him about how I helped you in the wilderness.

MOSES: While we were on our forty year trip through the wilderness, we became engaged in a battle with the Canaanite king of Arad and his army. We fought against them, and some of our people were taken hostage. We prayed to God for deliverance and our numbers were restored by God defeating the Canaanites. We then continued on our journey, but many of my followers became impatient and began cursing God and me. At that point, God called on you to come and bite them, and they died.

SERPENT: That was an ugly and repulsive job that I was called by God to do, but I did it because I serve God, and God knows what He wants done.

MOSES: Yes, you did it, and I am forever indebted to you for your saving me from that angry mob! Then, God had me pick you up and place you on a standard. God then decreed that those who had sinned and died from your bite, if they looked at you, they were restored to life again. Then, we continued on our way to the Promised Land. Thank you, Serpent, for guiding us, and I am sorry for hitting you so hard on the rock when God told me to strike the rock and receive water.

SERPENT: No problem I've been hit over the head many times since then. God has prescribed a special remedy to cure my aches and pains.

PHIL: I'm impressed! However, one time isn't the end of the world. What about all the other times you have caused problems?

SERPENT: You seem determined to blame me for every bad thing that happens. I can't help it if others do bad things. Remember, I am not God, I am only God's servant. Hezekiah, Hezekiah, will you come here and tell this space cadet what you observed happening to me and what you had to do about it?

HEZEKIAH: Oh, hello, Serpent! I still feel badly about what God had me do to you. I hope you have recovered. When I arrived on the spaceship, the people were worshiping you by placing you in the sacred place and burning incense to you. God told me that this was wrong and that I had to break the staff that you were on into pieces. In order to be faithful to God, I confess that I broke you into many pieces. My goodness, you appear to be well now.

SERPENT: Everything I am I owe to God!

PHIL: STOP! STOP! STOP! You are not getting off so easily! Just because you pulled off those few tricks, doesn't satisfy me. You haven't even apologized for your actions in misleading Eve.

GOD: I will take this one. Kid, just as I have placed you here on Spaceship Earth for a purpose, so I placed Serpent here also. I wanted Adam and Eve to die to Eden and to be born to Spaceship Earth, so I sent Serpent to inspire her to do more than live in the spirit. I wanted them to move on. However, Adam was so compliant and narrowly focused that he refused to mature and move on to greater challenges. You talked with him and heard him explain how long it took him to understand the mystery of the rocks. He was just getting to the thorns and the thistles. Can you guess how long it took me to get him sleeping in the house and not in the field? I almost had to send in a herd of turtles to get Adam's part of the story complete.

PHIL: So the serpent was sent to work out Adam's slowness in moving? That is a whole different message than I have understood before.

GOD: The serpent is inspiration, exaltation, and elevation to those who have the spirit to hear and respond. He is the Satan or devil to those who decide to replace me with their lies and deceptions. Remember how I told you to watch the plants and the animals on earth. You were to notice that they neither spin nor toil in their service to me. When you Earth cadets mess up, then I use one or more of them to save you from yourselves.

I want you to look to me for everything you need, and if you do so the possibilities for exploration throughout this spaceship and the other spaceships in the Universe I have created for you are endless. Enough of this I want you to go back and watch Adam struggle with and complete his first tasks on Spaceship Earth.

INTERPRETER: Phil is returned to observe and interact with Adam while wishing to stay and converse further with God.

PHIL: Here I am again. Did you miss me? How are your crops going? I hope you have all the rocks moved, I do not want to move any!

ADAM: You are just full of questions and comments, aren't you? No, I didn't miss you. Yes, the rocks are moved out of the field and the crops are fine, thank you so very much. I won't inconvenience you by asking for your help in the thistle and thorn fields. I know you must have a million things to learn and, anyway, if anyone is going to get credit for doing the work, I want it to be me!

PHIL: Adam, I'm sorry that I offended you. I will help you if you desire.

ADAM: No, this is my life story and the one that I received upon failing to answer God truthfully and for not taking the blame for my actions.

Anyway, I have grown to love the curse even more than I previously hated it. While I have been here, I have observed the mountains and the trees that grow in difficult places. They have spoken to me, telling me that their scars and twisted limbs are of no consequence when they commune with the stars. I have learned that my life has been constantly sheltered and feel shame that I have understood so little of my eternal walk with God.

I have also found true love with Eve, and now we are expecting our first child. I wouldn't exchange my life now for all the experiences that I had in the spiritual Eden before I wore this spacesuit.

PHIL: That all sounds so wonderful, but you still have to remove the thistles. How can you praise God as your feet, arms, legs, and hands bleed?

ADAM: Yes, I am bleeding even as you speak, yet I am seeing the seeds under each leaf and know that God has planted them there to inspire me to serve Him even when the task is painful. I am under this curse because I have not stayed true to everything in God's law and performed my appointed tasks perfectly. These thistles and thorns inspire me because they represent the thorns on God's head as He demonstrated His eternal saving grace in the space cadet man, Jesus.

PHIL: Wow! Do you think that I can find the seeds that God has placed for me in the prison where God has placed me? Is it possible that I have been looking too much at the razor wire fences, the guns and guards, the wardens, the inmates, and their crimes and possibly have overlooked seeing the seeds that God has placed there? Do you think that I just might be living my eternal life now and not be participating in it or learning to enjoy it?

ADAM: I think...

EVE: Adam! Adam, where are you? I have brought you lunch.

ADAM: Eve, you are so wonderful! I thought that you would not be doing that anymore since you are so full of our child. Sit down here and rest a while. Your face is very flushed, and you seem so tired.

INTERPRETER: Adam and Eve sit in a small area that has just been cleared of thorns and thistles.

EVE: Adam, you work so very hard and you have so many scratches on your beautiful body. I want to take oil and wash each cut and scratch so that they will heal. Oh! Oh! Adam, I just had a terrible pain in my belly and look, water is coming from me and I can't stop it. Adam, do something. Don't just sit there. Adam! Adam! Wake up! Don't fail me now. I think that the baby is coming, and this is no place to have a baby. Adam! Adam! O good, you finally came to. Will you please help me?!

ADAM: Eve, I don't know anything about babies. You tell me what you think I should do, and I will do it. Here lie down. Use this dead grass for your head. I hope the thorns and thistles don't stick you too much. Do you want me to carry you back to the house?

EVE: Yes, the thorns are sticking me. You can carry me back to the house. Oh no, there goes another one of those pains again. Get your hands off me! I am not going anywhere. This baby will be born right here in this damn field. God, be cursed for this day! Why didn't He let us know that the baby would be born now? God, if this pain is punishment for my deceit and falsehood, I am truly being punished for my crime! I am naked before Thee and am miserable because of the pain You are portioning out to me in abundance. The briars, the stinkweed, the thorns surround me and inflict Your punishment on my fragile body. God, why! Why! Why must I suffer so? Oh! Oh! There goes another awful pain. I can't bear it any longer!
Adam, damn it can't you do something! Adam! Adam! Where are You? O God NO, the wimp passed out again! All right serpent bite him on the heel again and get that no good mate of mine back into this horror show.

SERPENT: You got your wish. I don't think that your blood is going to concern Adam anymore. I just took a piece out of his heel. He is coming around now, and he looks like he is ready for a fight.

ADAM: Where's my club? I'll beat you bloody! You'll get your due now!

EVE: Adam! Get over here! I told the serpent to bite you, and if you pass out again...O O O O O O O O O O O O O O O O O O Adam, help me! Please Help me!!!!!!!!
Oh, God please help me! The pain is so terrible! Please forgive me! I am

so sorry God for blaming You for my sin. Please, God, please help me in my distress!

SERPENT: Eve, God has heard your cry for help, and sent me to help. You are God's child. You have always been forgiven by God's grace. Now, your earth suit can stretch no further. Please let me help you by telling you and Adam what to do to complete this delivery and give you some relief from your pain.

EVE: Adam, get that serpent out of here! I only want him here to bite you if you pass out again! He's the one that caused me all the trouble that I have been having. Get! Get, I tell you!

ADAM: Eve, maybe he can help us this time. After all, we are in a pretty difficult bind here. If he is to stay to bite me if I pass out, he may as well stay and give whatever advice he has to give. Serpent, are you here to help or to cause more trouble?

SERPENT: Eve called God for help and God sent me to give you some comfort and guidance. Do you want me to stay or leave?

THORNS AND THISTLES: Eve, we will help also. We will bear your pain as you deliver your babies. We are the saving grace of God sent to sacrifice ourselves for your pain. You will see that we can take all the anger and hurt from you and this moment will become a joy for you to cherish always.

INTERPRETER: By now Eve is having so much pain, she relents. The Serpent gives Adam instructions and the thorns and thistles draw the sin and pain from Eve's fragile body. Adam follows the directions as well as he is able, and soon the babies are delivered. Did I say babies? Yes, I said babies!

ADAM: Eve, look here! Oh, I forgot that you cannot look. Sorry. We not only have one baby, we have two. The second is coming along holding to the heal of the first. I guess he thinks that if he holds on he will get out quicker. Boy, does the first one look angry. Listen to him yell! The second one is so peaceful and happy. Eve, I am going to name the angry one Cain for he is raising a lot of cain with his noise. You name the second one.

EVE: The second one I name Abel because he will always be able to be happy and praise God as we have never been able to do. Maybe he will teach us how to love God in everything we do.

(SONG 6: CAST YOUR GRACE ON US)
O God, wash our sins away with thy dear blood.
We love Thee never before!
You who have borne our sins through the thorns You wore
Ever cast your grace on us.

Forever forbid me from boasting of my glee and joy
Which I now receive with these precious gifts given.
May I instead glory in Your passion for my sin
Which You have now removed with Your thorns entwined.

Praise all praise both Adam and I give to You.
Unworthy we be, yet privileged to be called your children.
May we ever serve and honor your acceptance and love
And teach our Cain and Abel the pure love we have received.

GOD: Kid, are you ready to begin your living on Spaceship Earth as I have created you? Do you understand that you may do anything you want to do and what that means for you and your fellow astronauts, peace and happiness? Can you forgive the wayward "want to's" of others?

PHIL: God, you already know my answers. Yes, I now desire to begin living as you expect me to live, but I am not as confident in me as you appear to be. I do want to share peace and happiness and to forgive others, yet I am mystified as to how to do that given the responsibility that you have entrusted me.
Would you teach me to forgive? Are there some whom You have taught this gift who do it well?

GOD: Yes, I will take you to people and places that I helped when I wore a spacesuit that you called Jesus.

JESUS: Hello, Phillip, would you care to walk with me as I care for some of my people and help you to understand forgiveness?

PHIL: WOW! You really are Jesus! Would I ever!!!!!! I will watch and try to learn. I promise to stay out of the way and not bother anyone.

JESUS: Quite the contrary, if you choose to talk with any of those whom I help, feel free to do so.

Here we are in my hometown of Nazareth. Look, a man is being brought on a cot who is paralyzed. Hello, sir why did you have these men bring you on your bed to me? What do you expect to happen?

CALACH: Master, You are so very good to speak to me, one who is so unworthy. I know of Your goodness and Your power of forgiveness. Master, I have sinned, I have disgraced Your trust in me, and I desire to serve You as You have ordered. Please forgive me of my sins!!!!

JESUS: Calach, your sins are forgiven, rise from your bed and go and live praising the purpose for which I formed you in the womb. May you and your family rejoice always!!!

PHIL: Hi, were you really paralyzed? Why? Why? Why did you come to Jesus? Didn't you know him as a young boy? Look at the others. They are scribes, and they think that Jesus is a fraud and a liar. Aren't you afraid of what might happen to you when Jesus leaves?

CALACH: I am here to serve God! I received forgiveness and am paralyzed no more. The scribes are able to do anything that they wish, and I shall serve the Lord my God. Here, see, I was on this bed, and now I carry it. Look around you. Do you think that those scribes could do anything with all these people praising God? Isn't it wonderful that God chose me to share His forgiveness with all my brothers and sisters?

JESUS: Come, Phillip, we have many lessons for you to learn. See these who are up ahead. They appear to be very angry and wish to harm me. You had better stay near so you will be safe.

Hello, my friends. May I help you in any way? Oh, I see you have a man here who bothers you because he is blind and unable to speak. Does he upset you?

CROWD: Yes, he upsets us. He is dirty, he smells, and he sits and pulls at our clothes as we pass by begging for money to buy his cheap wine to get drunk on. We want him gone from here, he's a disgrace to the neighborhood.

JESUS: Yaab, look at me and tell me about yourself!

YAAB: My Lord and my God, how I have prayed for you to come to me. Jesus, I worship the ground upon which you stand! You are so beautiful! The world is so beautiful! Praise be to God for the day You came to this place. I shall ever give thanks for your blessing me and forgiving me. I shall always look upon others as your blessed children.

PHARISEES: Hold it! Hold it! Wait just a minute! You are not welcome in this city. We do not need any satanic person here. We are having a difficult time just getting these no good sinners to bring their sacrifices of birds, grain, and sheep to the Temple. We don't need YOUR KIND here to cause problems. Either get out of here or we will have you arrested, you devil, you Satan person, you.

JESUS: You may call me whatever you desire. Sticks and stones will break my bones, but words will never hurt me. However, if you call my Spirit evil, you bear the sin of blasphemy, which shall be a scourge to you in this spaceship and on your next trip. You shall be a corruption on all whom you dominate. Your filthy words and beliefs will follow you all the days of your journey, and you will be despised by some, confused by others, and shunned by those who know and live the truth, such as this man who now sees and speaks.

Phillip, these men believe that flesh and blood is their main concern and if they follow legal rules and judge others by those rules as filthy or clean, then all life will be perfect. They have forgotten that they and all other people are my children and I am the cleansing soap. I have washed them clean by my word and now demonstrate this truth while I wear this garment. I don't expect you to understand what I am telling you now, so I want to take you on a little journey. Are you ready?

PHIL: Jesus, I'm just glad that we got away from that crowd. I don't know how that newly sighted man will survive in their midst. Whatever you are telling me will probably make sense sometime, but right now my mind is swirling with fear, with excitement, with awe for what is happening! Before we go on, please answer one question: Will they ever be forgiven?

JESUS: Phillip, those men have all the forgiveness of God in them that you have, but as long as they deny the truth, they will live and spread the lie. No one can serve two masters. Either he will love the one and hate the other or serve the one and despise the other. The lesson is here for you: Whom will you serve? Do you believe that God supplies all your needs? Has God formed you from the clay of creation and fashioned your spacesuit in the belly of your mother spacesuit factory, or are you a child of the god of lies and deceit, a god that exists only in men's fantastic imaginations and illusions.

PHIL: Jesus, You know my heart and my mind!!!!! I am Yours, and even though I may forget and sin against you, I want to be brought to my knees, asking forgiveness.

JESUS: Let's go on. You will think that I am leaving you for a while, but I never leave you. You will not see me for a while so that you can experience the final two portions of that prayer you have been trying to understand. See if you are able to discover the meaning of forgiveness and daily living that will test your faith in me and yourself. Remember, you have all the gifts of truth you need to succeed in this final learning exercise.

You are now watching an old Samaritan traveler who is walking with his donkey along a road from Jerusalem to Jericho. He has spent his life traveling while seeking the meaning of truth, love, and forgiveness. He lives humbly, professing that the world is his teacher. He listens at least twice as much as he speaks. He asks questions, anticipating that everyone he meets is a prophet. Phil, observe what happens now.

SHIMRAYTH: Mr. Donkey, I am glad that we are not in as much of hurry as those two men that just passed us. One of us probably would not survive. People are in too much of a rush these days. The world seems to be speeded up from when we were young. Everybody has to get to someplace yesterday. No time to stop and smell the roses.

Look, Mr. Donkey, what is that down in that ditch? Why if I'm not mistaken, it's a young lad. I hope he isn't dead. Let's take a look. My oh my, he has been beaten up and left to die in this ditch. I'll lift him up and lay him over your back. Sorry old friend, but you are stronger than I, so you'll have to carry him until we get to the next roadhouse.

Sir, my name is Shimrayth and my friend here is in bad repair. I want to rent a room from you for a few days to care for him. He must have been overtaken by rogues who beat him leaving him to die.

INNKEEPER: Is he any kin to you? Put your mark on this book, and my man will carry him to your room. I will have the girl bring some water and cloth to bandage his wounds.

SHIMRAYTH: No, I just found him, and he needed help. I thank you for your welcome. Here are two denarii for the time we will be spending here.

INTERPRETER: Shimrayth stays by the boy's side for several days and, seeing that an extended time will be needed for his healing, he takes two denarii to the innkeeper to pay for the boy's recovery. He tells the innkeeper that he will return within a week. Upon his return, the boy is much improved. Shimrayth pays the rest of the bill and places the boy on Mr. Donkey to return him to his home.

SHIMRAYTH: Young man, you look considerably more alive than you did just a few days ago. As soon as your leg heals, you will be as good as new. Tell me a little about yourself.

AYIN: My name is Ayin, and we live in the valley of olives and grapes. We produce much wine and the finest olives. My father's name is Telach, and my older brother's name is Jakech. After I left school, I wanted to see the world and to establish myself so that my father and brother would be proud of me. I asked my father for the money that would be coming to me at his death and he honored my foolish request.

SHIMRAYTH: Are you being disrespectful toward your father by calling him foolish? Son, I should have Mr. Donkey throw you off onto the ground right now for that thought!!! We Samaritans do not countenance to children disrespecting their elders!

AYIN: No, sir! I am in no way being disrespectful toward my father. He is a wonderful and honest man. He was so abundantly extravagant with me that he trusted me with all my inheritance even though I did not deserve it nor would I use it appropriately. He gave me the most wonderful blessing as I foolishly left home. Now, I just want to go back and work for him as one of his slaves.

SHIMRAYTH: Where did you travel and what did you do?

AYIN: I went east across the great river to a land that I had heard was full of promise. There, I met a man who had beautiful grain fields and fine barns. He was very old and wanted to sell them. I bought them and began to raise grain crops. The first year everything went so well that I had more crops than barns, so I began to tear down the smaller barns and replace them with bigger ones even though I saw many around me who were suffering from lack of grain and food. I decided to sell my grain and to drink and be merry. I neglected to feed the poor. I refused to present God with the best of my crop and to thank Him for my good fortune. God must have thought me the fool because the very next year, the rains did not come nor did the crops yield any grain. I was broken because I squandered the blessings that I had received. I lost the land because I could not even pay the taxes to the government.

I wandered the streets of the nearby city looking for food, and one day servants came through the streets inviting us to a big dinner given by their master. I went with them, and as we ate the master told us that he had invited his friends, relatives, and rich neighbors to thank them for their favors to him. All of these refused to come, so he invited us who were poor, crippled, lame, and blind. This was a true blessing from God! I wish that I had done the same.

SHIMRAYTH: What did you learn from your selfishness?

AYIN: I learned that God requires us to honor Him by loving our brothers and sisters and that we should not to be selfish with the blessings God gives us. After that, I went to work for a man who had many swine. I was filthy I was sure that God had decided to throw me overboard. I believed that since I had blasphemed my father by boldly asking for wealth that I had not earned and then had wasted it, I would die in the pig slop and no one would know or care that I had become swine food.

By the way, why did you stop to help a dirty, dying beggar? You know that others passed by and didn't help and people lie dying in ditches all the time. Why me?

SHIMRAYTH: I don't know really. When I looked at you I thought of myself when I was your age. I, too, went running off and wasted the Lord's blessings. I ran everywhere trying to find a way out of my dying ditch until a man came along. Who this man was I do not know. I only know that He picked me up and bandaged my wounds. No, He did more than bandage my wounds, He gave me peace in my heart and that has made all the difference. I was like a lost sheep, and He left all the rest of His flock and pulled me from my sure death.

Do you know what I mean when I tell you that regardless of what conditions I experience or where I sleep, I have a divine peace that glows inside me?

AYIN: I cannot truly say that I know what you are talking about. I am so angry at myself that I have profaned all the trust that was placed in me with my cursing, my carousing, my wastefulness, my...

SHIMRAYTH: Here, here, my boy! Now isn't the time to look back. Now is the time to look forward. I imagine that your father and brother are waiting night and day along the road for your return. Is it not possible that they are worried to death about your safety? Maybe God heard their prayers and sent me to pluck you from that terrible grave.

AYIN: AYIN Stop! Stop this minute! You know my father, don't you? He sent you to find me and bring me home so that he could get back at me for wasting his money. Didn't he?

SHIMRAYTH: Son, you may believe me or not, but I have never been in this province before. After all, I am a Samaritan and your people have no dealings with my kind. When I get you near your home, I will have to let you off Mr. Donkey and disappear because they will believe that I am holding you for ransom. I would probably be killed before you could even tell the story of what happened.

AYIN: I'm sorry. See, there I go being suspicious. I pray that I may someday have the kindness and love you have in your heart. I am so grateful for you for saving my life! Please forgive me.

Look! Up ahead, there is my father's house! Look who is coming! It is father! I shall run to him and submit myself to him as his slave.

Father, I have sinned before you and before God. I am no longer worthy to be called your son. Please let me serve you as one of your lowliest slaves all the days of my life.

TELACH: My son! My son, you were dead and now you live! You have returned to me. My prayers are answered. Quick, servants, bring a robe. No, wear mine. Give me your hand. Here is my ring. Let me place on your feet these sandals. Kill the fatted calf, invite all the friends, for my son was dead and now he is alive again. He was lost and now he is found! Let the celebration begin! May the trumpeters blow their horns and the drummers drum, may everyone rejoice! Come one, come all!

AYIN: Father, did you not hear me? I squandered your fortune. I wasted your trust and faith in me. I am not worthy to be your son.

TELACH: My son, you are my son not because you are frugal, loyal, submissive, wasteful, or a squanderer. You are my son because I made you. I shall always be your father, and you shall always be my son. I am the prodigal because I shall always be extravagant with you and all my children. I shall be reckless with my love to the degree that I shall love you when you are unloving to me or anyone else. I shall unceasingly die for you even though you do not understand my dying. I shall waste everything so that you may have the knowledge that I am your home and so that you will desire to live in me even if you do not understand. I desire only that you and all my children shall want to live with me always, for I am the source of all supply.

(SONG 8: SO IS THY COMING)
O God, I praise you, dear Lord,
With thanksgiving for Your wonderful gift.
For Your love outpoured on me this day,
For family restored, I praise You, Lord.
I praise You. I praise You, Lord.
With all my heart I praise Your holy name.

The Lord is never far away
But, through all grief distressing
An ever present help and stay,
Our peace and blessing.

As with a mother's tender hand,
He leads His own, His chosen band.

Thank You, my God, for all Your gifts,
For wondrous things that You have done
Forgive me O Lord, for my doubt and grief.
You are my strength. I praise You, Lord.
I praise You. I praise You, Lord.
With all my heart I praise Your holy name.
I breathe right now the great Amen!

INTERPRETER: Ayan watches as his father runs jubilantly to the house. He then turns toward Shimrayth.

AYIN: Shimrayth, my father couldn't see you or Mr. Donkey, could he? I know that you are not coming to the celebration, are you? My friend, please don't leave me! You have helped me to learn of myself and my purpose for being here. Shimrayth, I love you!!!!!!!

SHIMRAYTH: My dear friend yes, I must leave now and you must go from here facing each day as you have learned to live these past few days. You are well now. Go in peace. Ayin, I love you so very much, and I shall never let you out of my heart!!!!

INTERPRETER: Shimrayth disappears from sight and reappears as God's presence.

GOD: You don't look like the boy that began this journey. Have you learned why I brought you to this spaceship and what I want you to do while you are a space cadet here?

PHIL: I have learned that all the cadets here, including myself, have been chosen by You to be here. I have learned that the tasks that you give us are not temptations to screen out the winners from the losers, but challenges for us. These challenges will test our perseverance and our faith. Some of these challenges we will approach with great joy and glee, even imagining we are in heaven. Others will almost consume us and appear hellish and damnable. However, all will be opportunities to serve You and our fellow astronauts by putting our faith into action.

GOD: Boy, you may be a slow learner, but when you learn, you can really spout it out! Now, do you know where you are going to go?

PHIL: I guess that I will be a little like Dorothy, except instead of Kansas, I'll be back in Illinois back with my beautiful bride and back with the people in the prison.

GOD: Right you are! You are back in the twenty-first century. I hope you remember what you have learned.

INTERPRETER: Phil cannot wait to tell everyone what he has learned. The first one he meets should be careful because he's going to get an earful.

PHIL: Hi, Louis! Boy, have I got a great story to tell you! You won't believe where I have been, what I have seen, and what I have learned!

LOUIS: That will just have to wait a minute!!! I now know what has been going on in my life. I have been in a great test to help me learn about myself and why I am here on Earth. I have learned that lending my keys to someone to use my car was the beginning of a trip that I would never have wished on my worst enemy, but while on this trip, I have experienced a relationship with God that I never could have imagined.

Even though I am guilty of no crime, I have gone through the court system, been found guilty, have been stripped, searched, photographed, and humiliated. I have learned how many live and suffer silently. I have learned that one must arm himself with the knowledge that both God and man gives him. I have learned not only how to survive in terrible conditions, but how to grow through them.

I have learned to love men whom I would hardly speak to outside the prison. I have worked with a great and wonderful teacher who has helped thousands of convicted criminals not only to read and write, but to know that they are respected and honored as God's children. I have seen an eighty-one-year-old man learn to write his name, learn to read and to do mathematics so that he can have a better chance to make it in the world. I have learned that I can teach people who really need education to prosper in the world. I have learned that God has many things for me to do when I am freed from this incarceration.

The best learning that I have acquired is the knowledge that I have an eternal calling to serve God with all my talents, whether in this prison or in my community or wherever God calls me to go. Now, what were you going to tell me?

PHIL: I just wanted to say, "I'VE GOT TO GET STARTED! GOOD NIGHT, FOLKS AND GOD BLESS YOU, EVERYONE!"

(SONG 9: SING PRAISE REPRISE)

Overture

Rebecca Watts

You Are

Rebecca Watts

2

Sing Praise

Animals in Eden

Rebecca Watts

Song of the Birds

The Serpent is a Servant of God

Rebecca Watts

Cast Your Grace on Us

So Is Thy Coming

195

2

Sing Praise

2

The Lord is ne - ver far a - way but, through all grief dis - tress- ing an e - ver pre - sent help and stay, our peace and bles - sing.

As with a mo - ther's ten - der hand He leads his own, his cho - sen band.

I breathe right now the great A - men!

CPSIA information can be obtained at www.ICGtesting.com
Printed in the USA
LVOW11s0824060214

372511LV00002B/150/P